Samuel Sharpe, Joseph Bonomi, Francis Frith

Egypt, Nubia and Ethiopia

Samuel Sharpe, Joseph Bonomi, Francis Frith

Egypt, Nubia and Ethiopia

ISBN/EAN: 9783337330132

Printed in Europe, USA, Canada, Australia, Japan

Cover: Foto ©ninafisch / pixelio.de

More available books at **www.hansebooks.com**

EGYPT, NUBIA,

AND

ETHIOPIA.

ILLUSTRATED BY ONE HUNDRED STEREOSCOPIC PHOTOGRAPHS,

TAKEN BY

FRANCIS FRITH FOR Messrs. NEGRETTI AND ZAMBRA;

WITH DESCRIPTIONS

AND NUMEROUS WOOD ENGRAVINGS,

BY JOSEPH BONOMI, F.R.S.L., AUTHOR OF "NINEVEH AND ITS PALACES;"

AND NOTES

BY SAMUEL SHARPE, AUTHOR OF "THE HISTORY OF EGYPT."

LONDON:
SMITH, ELDER AND CO., 65, CORNHILL.

M.DCCC.LXII.

TO

HIS GRACE THE DUKE OF NORTHUMBERLAND,

K.G., D.C.L., F.R.S., ETC. ETC. ETC.,

THE EGYPTIAN TRAVELLER,

THE PATRON OF EGYPTIAN AND ARABIC STUDIES,

AND

THE GENEROUS CONTRIBUTOR TO THE EGYPTIAN COLLECTION

IN THE BRITISH MUSEUM,

This Work

IS RESPECTFULLY DEDICATED,

BY HIS OBEDIENT SERVANTS,

NEGRETTI AND ZAMBRA.

PREFACE.

The valley of the Nile has been visited by a variety of travellers, who have brought home drawings of the buildings made under various difficulties. Denon, following the French army, published a volume of views; but too often sketched hastily, perhaps while his comrades were engaged in battle. The scientific expedition sent out by Napoleon was accompanied by several artists; but their costly volumes too clearly show that the drawings received many of their last touches in Paris. Some of our English artists have also published beautiful volumes of the picturesque ruins in this land, most interesting for the draftsman; but we cannot but sometimes fancy that they have sacrificed somewhat of scientific accuracy to artistic effect. But when we look at Photographic views, we are troubled by no such misgivings. Here we have all the truthfulness of nature, all the reality of the objects themselves, and, at the same time, artistic effects which leave us nothing to wish for.

The following sun-pictures of the ancient ruined buildings on the banks of the Nile were made for Messrs. Negretti and Zambra by Mr. Frith, during a visit to Egypt, Nubia and Ethiopia, in the years 1859, 1860. They are one hundred in number. Every view is of two pictures almost the same, but not quite so. They are taken by two instruments at the same time, and not quite from the same spot. One is a view as seen by the right eye, and one as seen by the left eye. If we are looking at a round object, as at the nearest column in Plate XLVII., one view shows us a little more of one side of the column, and the other of the other side. But the difference is so little that it is not easily noted. If, however, the reader examines with a microscope how much of any figure on the second column is hid by the first, he will clearly see that the two views are not quite the same. In order to observe the effect gained by our having these two views of one object, we must look at them through the stereoscope or double eye-glass. By means of this, each eye looks at its own picture; and the two pictures thus seen at the same time are carried separately by the optic nerves to the brain, where they meet as one; and we then see every object on the flat paper as if it were solid. Every object seems raised into full relief, and for the same reason that an object, a really solid, is seen to be so,—because the two eyes have different views of it. Every line in one picture is distant from the same line in the other picture by about two inches and thirteen sixteenths of an inch, which is the distance in most persons between the two eyes.

Though we often lay a picture down on the table when we look at it, yet it has been drawn in every case, with very rare exceptions, as if it were to be placed against the wall, or held upright. The laws of perspective are framed for pictures that represent the natural views when they are placed upright. Hence the photographer places his instrument so that the chemically prepared plate, upon which the picture is to be formed, may stand upright; and then the upright lines in the buildings are upright in his picture, while the horizontal lines in the buildings all point to certain spots on the horizon, called the vanishing points. But

PREFACE.

in the case of the figures in front of the rock temples of Abou Simbel, in Nubia, seen in our Plates LXXVIII., LXXIX. and LXXXIII., this rule could not easily be followed. They are too near the river's edge. The artist must have had a frame raised in the middle of the river, if he would have shown the front view of these temples in the usual way. Hence he has been obliged to slope his instrument upwards, and has given some rather unusual pictures. They are not formed according to the usual laws of perspective. The lines which are upright in nature are not parallel in the picture, but drawn towards a distant point, as may be seen in Plate LXXIX. If this plate is held upright, the temple seems to be sloping backwards, and the colossal figure of the queen almost lying on the ground. If we would see it as in nature, we must hold it overhead, and let it slope forwards. The explanation seemed necessary as an apology for those Plates; while their very peculiarity may be made use of to explain the laws of perspective.

The series of views is arranged geographically from north to south. We begin with Cairo and the Pyramids, and, following the course of the river, we proceed to Dendera, to Thebes, to Hermonthis, to Philæ and Biggeh, at the first cataract, where we quit Egypt and enter Nubia; and then on to Abou Simbel, at the second cataract, examining the principal buildings as we pass. This takes us to our sixty-second view. After this the ruins become less frequent and less important, and our last view finds us at the temple of Soleb, in Ethiopia, beyond the stony district of the second cataract.

The age of the several buildings which we are looking at is very various. Overlooking the huts of the present inhabitants of Egypt, seen in Plate XC., and the modern city of Cairo,

PREFACE.

built about one thousand years ago, we have ruined ancient temples of four great epochs. We begin with the Pyramids near Memphis, which are the oldest buildings in the world. These were built by the kings of Lower Egypt. For the great Theban kings, we have the temples of Upper Egypt and Nubia, built before the Hebrew nation had established its monarchy under David. For the Greek kings, the Ptolemies, whose line ended with Cleopatra, we have the temples of Philæ and Hermonthis; and for the Roman emperors we have Kalabshe and Dabod. These temples are all of the old Egyptian style, and so far alike that at one time they were thought to be all of nearly the same age; and it was only within the present century, after the hieroglyphics had been read by Dr. Young and M. Champollion, that the difference in their age has been learned. By the hieroglyphical writing upon them we are now able to study the progress of the nation in art and civilization, at first from worse to better, but afterwards, unfortunately, from better to worse.

The history of some nations is written in their wars and conquests, of other nations, in their literature; but in the case of Egypt, as distinguished from Alexandria, its history is to be studied in its noble buildings, its tombs, made in imitation of mountains; its temples hollowed out of the rock, and its rocks shaped into colossal statues. Of these the reader here has a series of views which cannot be but faithful. The descriptions of them are by Mr. Joseph Bonomi, whose residence of twelve years in the country, and continued attention to Egyptian art, entitle his words to our full confidence.

S. S.

CONTENTS.

PLATE		PAGE
I.	The Mosque of Sultan Hassan—Cairo	1
II.	Cairo, and distant View of Pyramids	5
III.	The Pyramids of Gizeh	7
IV.	The Great Pyramid and Head of Sphinx	11
V.	Gizeh during the Inundations	13
VI.	The Quarries of Toura, and Pyramids	15
VII.	Sioat, or Lycopolis	17
VIII.	Temple of Dendera	19
IX.	Errebek—Thebes	21
X.	The Temple of Errebek—Thebes	23
XI.	The Temple of Errebek—Portico	25
XII.	The Temple of Errebek—Entrance to Sanctuary	27
XIII.	The Memnonium—Thebes	29
XIV.	The Memnonium—Near View of the Columns	33
XV.	Osiride Columns of the Memnonium	35
XVI.	The Fallen Colossus of the Memnonium	39
XVII.	Foundations of the Temple near Dayr-el-Bahree—Thebes	43
XVIII.	Buildings and Rocks near Dayr-el-Bahree	45
XIX.	The Plain of Thebes, with New Excavations	47
XX.	The Temple near Dayr-el-Medineh	49
XXI.	The Two Colossal Statues of Memnon—Thebes	51
XXII.	The Temple of Medinet-Habou—Thebes	57
XXIII.	The Temple of Medinet-Habou—Near View	61
XXIV.	Osiride Columns of the Temple of Medinet-Habou	63

CONTENTS.

PLATE		PAGE
XXV.	Near View of Osiride Columns of the Temple of Medinet-Habou	65
XXVI.	New Excavations of Medinet-Habou	67
XXVII.	The Temple of Luxor—Thebes.—The Obelisk	69
XXVIII.	The Temple of Luxor—Thebes. Head of Colossal Statue near the Entrance	73
XXIX.	The Temple of Karnak, Thebes—Central Avenue	75
XXX.	Columns and Part of the Obelisk of Thothmosis II.—Karnak, Thebes	77
XXXI.	Columns of the Temple of Karnak, Thebes	81
XXXII.	Hall of the Temple of Karnak, Thebes	83
XXXIII.	Temple of Karnak.—View from the Top of Hall	87
XXXIV.	Temple of Karnak: with Colonnade	93
XXXV.	Temple of Karnak.—Columns with Capitals in Imitation of full-blown Papyrus	97
XXXVI.	Temple of Karnak.—Columns with Capitals in Imitation of Papyrus Bud	99
XXXVII.	The fallen Obelisk, and the Obelisk of Thothmosis II. at Karnak	101
XXXVIII.	Side View of the Obelisk at Karnak	105
XXXIX.	Karnak	107
XL.	The Temple of Erment or Hermonthis	111
XLI.	Part of the Temple of Koum Ombos	115
XLII.	The Temple of Koum Ombos	117
XLIII.	The Temple of Koum Ombos—the Portico	119
XLIV.	Columns at Koum Ombos, with Composite Capitals	121
XLV.	Fallen Architrave of Koum Ombos	123
XLVI.	Columns at Koum Ombos with Capitals of full-blown Papyrus	125
XLVII.	Columns at Koum Ombos with Palm-leaf Capitals	127
XLVIII.	View through the Portico at Koum Ombos	129
XLIX.	General View of Koum Ombos	131
L.	Sandstone Quarries at Hager Silsilis	133
LI.	Sandstone Quarries at Hager Silsilis—General View	135

CONTENTS.

PLATE		PAGE
LII.	Assouan, or Syene	137
LIII.	The Temples on the Island of Philæ	139
LIV.	Temples on the Island of Philæ—Entrance	141
LV.	Temples on the Island of Philæ—the great Pylon	143
LVI.	Colonnade of the great Courtyard of the Temple of Philæ	145
LVII.	The smaller Temple of Philæ	147
LVIII.	Entrance to the small Temple of Philæ	149
LIX.	View from the Roof of the small Temple of Philæ	151
LX.	View of the Nile from Philæ	153
LXI.	Ruins on the Island of Biggeh	155
LXII.	Roman Arch on the Island of Biggeh	157
LXIII.	The Temple of Dabod in Nubia	159
LXIV.	Interior of the Temple of Dabod	161
LXV.	The Temple of Kardassy—Nubia	163
LXVI.	Tablets in the Quarries at Kardassy	165
LXVII.	The Temple of Kalabshe	167
LXVIII.	Interior of the Temple of Kalabshe	171
LXIX.	Temple of Kalabshe: Second Entrance	173
LXX.	The Temple of Dandour	175
LXXI.	The Temple of Gerf	177
LXXII.	The Temple at Dakkeh	179
LXXIII.	The Temple at Maharraka—General View	181
LXXIV.	The Temple of Maharraka—Side View	183
LXXV.	Wady Sebouah, from the West	185
LXXVI.	View at Wady Sebouah	187
LXXVII.	The Temple of Wady Sebouah—General View	189
LXXVIII.	The small Rock Temple at Abou Simbel	191
LXXIX.	Colossal Figure of the Queen at the small Temple at Abou Simbel.	193
LXXX.	The Great Rock Temple of Abou Simbel	195
LXXXI.	Entrance to the Great Rock Temple at Abou Simbel	199

CONTENTS.

PLATE		PAGE
LXXXII.	Colossal Statue of Rameses, Abou Simbel	201
LXXXIII.	Western Figure on the Great Rock Temple at Abou Simbel	203
LXXXIV.	The Cataract of Samneh—Ethiopia	207
LXXXV.	The Temple of Samneh	209
LXXXVI.	The Temple at Samneh—from the East	211
LXXXVII.	Near View of the Temple at Samneh	213
LXXXVIII.	Northern Portion of the Temple at Samneh	215
LXXXIX.	Island of Abd e' Sour	217
XC.	Encampment under a Doum Palm	219
XCI.	The Cataract of Tangour—Ethiopia	221
XCII.	Cotton-Spinning at Kolbe—Ethiopia	223
XCIII.	Wady Furket	225
XCIV.	Columns of the Temple at Amara—Ethiopia	227
XCV.	Near View of the Columns of the Temple at Amara—Ethiopia	229
XCVI.	Granite Columns on the Island of Sayo—Ethiopia	231
XCVII.	Column of Amunothph III. at Soleb—Ethiopia	233
XCVIII.	General View of Columns of Amunothph III. at Soleb	235
XCIX.	View of the Column of Amunothph III. at Soleb, from the East	237
C.	Soleb, looking from the Inner Court towards the Gate	239

PLATE I.

The Mosque of Sultan Hassan—Cairo.

THE modern capital of Egypt abounds with beautiful specimens of that offshoot of Roman architecture, which the Italians call Saracenico; and perhaps there is not any city in the world of the size of Cairo that can boast of so many public buildings; for mosques, schools, bazaars, khans, sebeels, and baths are to be found in every quarter. That particular branch of Saracenic architecture which attained to such great perfection in Egypt seems to have been imported by the Mohammedan invaders in the 7th century, and to have risen to its greatest splendour at the end of the 13th, and beginning of the 14th centuries, at which period were built those beautiful mosque tombs now crumbling to decay in the desert plains to the north and south of the city. From the 14th century down to the reign of Mohammed Ali, the head of the present dynasty, this beautiful style of architecture seems to have gradually declined, and it is now entirely superseded by the Turkish. All the larger buildings which have been erected at Cairo within these thirty years are in a mawkish style, a mixture of Chinese and Italian, imported from Constantinople. It began in the palace built for Toussoun Pasha, and has, as it were, taken root in the very citadel, in the costly structure of marble from the quarries of Alabastron which Mohammed Ali erected, in a true Hametic spirit, for his own sepulchre.

The ease and unrestricted grace with which the Egyptian branch of the Saracenic adapts itself to the requirements of the climate and the destination of the structure, is exhibited in some of the older houses in various quarters of the city, which are perfect models of its adaptability to the domestic arrangements of both the Christian and Mohammedan inhabitants.

I.—THE MOSQUE OF SULTAN HASSAN—CAIRO.

Amongst the mosque tombs, perhaps that called Cubut el Howar is the most gorgeous specimen of painted architectural decoration, not surpassed by any chamber in the Alhambra. This tomb is not one of the group outside the Bab Ennasser, but stands alone on an elevation on the road to Materieh, the Heliopolis of the Septuagint. It is called Cubut el Howar, or the Cupola of the Winds, from its exposed and dilapidated condition making it accessible to the wind from whatever quarter. In its cupola is a hole made by a cannon ball during some skirmish on the spot between the French and the Mamelukes.

In the view before us, which is taken from the roof of some of the government workshops at the base of the citadel, are two fine examples of the Saracenic style as adapted to a sacred structure. The edifice to the left is the mosque or elgama Sultan Hassan. It was built by the second Sultan of that name, A.D. 1361. The French architects who accompanied the first Napoleon considered it to be the finest specimen of masonry in Cairo. The mosque in its greatest length measures 160 yards, and the height of the tallest minaret 65 yards. In the interior is a beautiful frieze of sculptured writing in the Cufic or ancient Arabic character, interspersed with flowers. This mode of decoration is as marked a feature in the Saracenic style as is the sculptured frieze in the Greek and Roman, and to some minds it is superior to mere ornament, however elaborate, of reiterated festoons and scrolls; for while it delights the eye it appeals to the understanding, therefore, ranking next to the frieze of sculptured figures, which records some event or teaches some moral. Another characteristic of this style is that the general outline is not disturbed by the ornamentation; there are no projecting cornices or mouldings, but all the decoration is cut in out of the solid. The particular example of the Mosque Sultan Hassan presents a remarkable exception to this rule in the oppressive cornice which disfigures the structure. To our right is the mosque called Jama el Mamoudyeh, neither so large nor of such excellent masonry as that just described, but far superior in point of design. The form of the cupola is more graceful, and the way it grows out of the cubical base is a feature of great beauty, this mode of transition from the cube to the cylinder being peculiar to the style. The construction by which

I.—THE MOSQUE OF SULTAN HASSAN—CAIRO.

the development of the cylinder is attained, is best seen in the interior. The corners of the cube are gradually filled up by a succession of small arches which are multiplied in every succeeding course until the square becomes a circle, out of which the cupola rises. This mode of structure is of eastern origin, found to exist in some ancient tombs in the Crimea.

On the very top of the minarets of Sultan Hassan may be seen the wooden frame on which are hung the lamps that light up the city during the Ramadan, and which every minaret should be provided with. In the open space, called the Kara maidan, before the mosque may be distinguished the busy crowd. On certain days of the week a cattle market is held in this open space, and every day, in the cool of the afternoon, may be seen, just where the crowd is, under the smaller minaret, a public reciter chanting to the sound of a violin with one string, the romance of Abu Zeit, or enlivening the pauses of a story in the Arabian Nights with a note or two from the same extraordinary instrument. The reciter sits on the ground, and is surrounded by a picturesque group of listeners. The naked children sitting on the ground, or on their mothers' shoulders; the donkey boy with his ass; the Turkish soldier; the Greek; the Copt; the half-naked water-carrier; the camel driver; the Arab of the desert, with his bournous over his mouth; the robust Fellah, with his nabout or long staff, and the seller of bread with his tray. A little farther to the right passing close to the smaller minaret is the Suke es sillah, or market for arms, in which street is the grand entrance to the mosque, a masterpiece of elaborate ornament. Farther on are some Turkish palaces, the residences of persons in authority, and beyond these the more picturesque dwellings of the commonalty; then the Nile, and at last the horizontal line of the Lybian desert.

J. B.

NOTE.—Alexandria was besieged and taken by the Arabs in A.D. 640, when they were at once masters of all Egypt, and the last remains of the Greek power in the country came to an end. The first seat of their government

I.—THE MOSQUE OF SULTAN HASSAN—CAIRO.

was at Babylon, a fortress on the right bank of the Nile opposite to Memphis. The town around this fortress, when in their hands, received the name of Cairo, and then of Old Cairo, when the present city of Cairo was built as the Arabic capital of Egypt about A.D. 970.

The eastern half of the Delta had at all times been in part peopled by Jews, Phœnicians, and Arabs, who quietly settled there and mixed with the Egyptian population, as the western half of the Delta had been sprinkled with Greek settlers. And hence arose the reason for building the capital in that neighbourhood; and never was a city built more at the expense of its neighbours. If we now look round the Delta and inquire where are the temples of Memphis, where are the sculptured casing stones of the pyramids, we find that they were pulled down to build the city of Cairo. If we seek for the remains of the temple of Heliopolis, where Plato went to study, they are to be seen in the walls of Cairo. If we would study the architecture of the great temple of Serapis, the pride of Alexandria, we must examine the columns which now uphold the mosques of Cairo. Four hundred Greek columns from Alexandria now ornament one of these Mohamedan mosques.

S. S.

PLATE II.

Cairo, and Distant View of Pyramids.

THIS view is taken from a still greater elevation than the last, from the top of a house, probably in the citadel. Nearly in the centre of the picture the three great pyramids of Gizeh break the horizontal line of the Lybian desert; and below the second the head of the Sphinx is just discernible. More to the left, over Old Cairo, the Nile is seen; and in the barren plain, between the river and the most distant houses, a faint streak marks out the direction of the aquaduct which conveys water to the ancient well of the citadel. To the right is one of those artificial mounds, the accumulation of the rubbish of the city which, like the Monte Testaccio of Rome, is chiefly composed of broken pottery; then the houses of the south-western quarter of the city, among which, intersected by a minaret, is a white building in the Turkish style, a palace of the late Ibrahim Pasha. Conspicuously prominent in the foreground is one of those contrivances called a malakef, a sloping shed of boards directed towards the north or north-west, to arrest and conduct to an open apartment below, the cool breezes which generally blow from those quarters. In the present example the side planks are wanting.

J. B.

PLATE III.

The Pyramids of Gizeh.

"Then had I been at rest, with kings and counsellors of the earth, which built desolate places for themselves:" Job iii., 14. Whether the writer of these words ever saw or heard of this vast desert plain strewn with the most ancient, the most costly, and the largest and most durable tombs ever devised by the art of man, may be matter of doubt; but certainly there is no spot on the earth to which those words so aptly apply, and with so much force from the greatest antiquity down to the present moment, as to this desert of Gizeh. There is not, in all the world besides, a continuous cemetery fifty miles in extent. There is not, in all the world besides, a spot where there are so many costly and solid structures, which the kings and counsellors of the earth have built for themselves during their own lives. Not after death or by others were their monuments erected, as was that celebrated tomb which Queen Artemisia built for Mausolus, her husband; but for and by themselves in these desolate plains of Gizeh. It was the custom in Egypt for the "kings and counsellors," and those who could afford to build at all, to build their own tombs, and in a more solid form than the buildings occupied by them while living; and the site they chose was always in the desert land on the western side of the Nile. To this circumstance of building the tomb during life, is attributed the great dimensions of the larger pyramids of Gizeh, which are the tombs of kings whose reigns were both longer and more prosperous than were those of the other kings whose resting-places lie contiguous in the same desolate place. The view before us is taken from the cultivatable plain to the south of the pyramids, and the dark, black alluvium contrasts strongly with the desert sand. On the right is the largest pyramid; then follows that which is called the second pyramid. Still on the upper part of this second largest building in the world, is a

III.—THE PYRAMIDS OF GIZEH.

piece of the casing, which is made of a fine kind of limestone brought from the quarries on the eastern side of the Nile. To climb over this crust and attain to the summit is a difficult and dangerous task; accordingly there are persons found, even in this desert of Gizeh, who are ready and willing to give money to see a poor inhabitant of a neighbouring village risk his life in so doing, just as in populous London, persons, who esteem themselves still more civilized, are willing to pay to see a man risk his life on a tight rope at the Crystal Palace. The whole of this crust or casing has been removed from the greater pyramid, and from the lower part of the second, these monuments having served as quarries for all the stone constructions in the province of Gizeh and its neighbourhood, certainly ever since the conquest of the country by the Mohammedans, if not before that time.

J. B.

NOTE.—The largest pyramid, in which was found the name of Nef-chofo (see fig. 1), is about 764 feet wide, and 500 feet high.

The second pyramid, in which was found the name of Chofo (see fig. 2), is about 707 feet wide, and 460 feet high.

The third pyramid, in which was found the name of Mykera (see fig. 3), is about 354 feet wide. In all the proportion between the half of the base and the height is as eight to ten.

Herodotus tells us that the largest pyramid is the oldest, and that it was built by Cheops, and that the second in age and in size was built by Chephren. But since these buildings have been opened, we have learned to distrust his information. Several circumstances agree in leading us to think that the largest pyramid is not so old as that which is second in size. First, the hieroglyphical name of the king who built the larger pyramid is Nef-chofo (fig. 1), while Chofo (fig. 2) is the name of the builder of the smaller; and we naturally suppose that the simpler name is older than the compound name, which is formed from it. Secondly, the causeway by which the stones were brought to the high ground upon which the pyramid

Fig. 1.   Fig. 2.

III.—THE PYRAMIDS OF GIZEH.

stands, has a bend in it. It would seem as if it first led directly to the pyramid of Chofo, and was afterwards turned towards that of Nef-chofo, and hence that Chofo's pyramid was the older of the two. Thirdly, the passages and chambers in the pyramid of Nef-chofo are complicated, and show more forethought and design as to keeping safe the body which was to be buried; hence, again, we may suppose that Chofo's pyramid with its one chamber and simpler passage is the older. Fourthly, as the ambitious aim of the builders is sufficiently clear, it is not easy to suppose that the second builder modestly planned that his pyramid should be forty feet less high than that of his predecessor; he surely meant to outshine that which was already built, and to make his building forty feet the highest. These several reasons are quite enough to prove that the pyramid of Nef-chofo, which is the largest of the two, was built after that of Chofo.

The age of the pyramids cannot be fixed with certainty. They may have been built 1700 years before the Christian era, or they may be much older. They can hardly be more modern; they are at the same time the oldest and the largest buildings in the world. Manetho, the historian, tells us that Queen Nitocris, the builder of the third pyramid, was the twelfth, in order of succession, of the sovereigns of Memphis after the builder of the oldest pyramid. Now, if Nitocris was the wife of Thothmosis II., whose successor, Thothmosis III. was the Menophra, who gave his name to the era of B.C. 1322, when the Sothic period began, we have the oldest pyramid built thirteen reigns, or about 350 years before the year B.C. 1322.

Fig. 3.

The third pyramid, and the fourth, a small one that stands beside it, both contain the name King Mykera as the builder. (Fig. 3). Now, as the first name of Queen Nitocris was Mykera, that may have been also one of the names of her Theban husband; and being like him a sovereign in her own right, she perhaps built one for him and one for herself.

A work of art in order to be sublime must not startle us, or take us by surprise. On the other hand, it should raise our expectations step by step, and make us admire it more and more, the more we are acquainted with it. And if after thorough examination and full acquaintance, we find

III.—THE PYRAMIDS OF GIZEH.

that our raised expectations, instead of being disappointed, have been fully satisfied, and we then acknowledge the grandeur of the work, it is because the artist has produced something which is truly sublime. Such are the pyramids of Gizeh. The traveller sees them in the distance, even from Cairo. He crosses the Nile, and rides towards them over the plain. They rise in height, their outline becomes more marked, and when he reaches the base of the nearest, he looks up in astonishment and awe. He has had his wonder raised higher every step as he approached it, and when he arrives at its foot, he feels no disappointment, his expectations are fully satisfied. The sublime in art can hardly do more.

S. S.

The god Amun Ra putting life into the mouth of King Thothmosis III.

PLATE IV.

The Great Pyramid, and Head of Sphinx.

In the foreground of this picture are some new excavations which have laid bare certain ancient galleries cut in the living rock and covered by large well-squared blocks. These subterranean galleries very much resemble those opened by Colonel Vyse, and called by him "Campbell's Tomb." Beyond is the head of the Sphinx, which is the recumbent statue of a lion with a human head, and carved out of the numulitic rock on which the Pyramids stand, and of which their chief bulk consists. This huge statue is buried up to the top of its back in the encroaching sands of the Lybian desert. Farther in the distance is the great Pyramid showing its southern and eastern sides, and the three small pyramids contiguous. These small pyramids were opened by Colonel Vyse, and since his time all the blocks of fine limestone which lined the chambers of these structures have been removed. There is a manufactory of stone mortars for pounding indigo constantly going on, and as the mortars are made out of the fine limestone of all these ancient buildings (besides what is broken up and carried away for mending the dykes and bridges of a whole province), the extent of the destruction may easily be imagined.

J. B.

NOTE.—The colossal Sphinx, of which the head is here seen by the side of the largest pyramid, that of Nef-chofo, lies in front of the oldest pyramid, that of Chofo, which is second in size. It was in all probability made at the same time as Chofo's pyramid, to which it is an ornament. Between its fore paws is a small temple, added, perhaps, four centuries

IV.—THE GREAT PYRAMID, AND HEAD OF SPHINX.

afterwards, and bearing the name of Thothmosis IV. (see fig. 5), who is there represented as worshipping this huge monster. Thothmosis IV. lived about B.C. 1270.

Fig. 4.

Fig. 4 represents the Sphinx and the small temple, when the sand was removed from around it by Captain Caviglia in 1817.

Fig. 5.

The three small pyramids on the east side of the great pyramid each stand upon an aroura of land, or half an acre.

S. S.

PLATE V.

Gizeh during the Inundations.

For three months in the year the villages and towns of this remarkable country become islands or promontories, joined to the desert, or to some town nearer to the banks of the river, by an artificial dyke. This artificial dyke serves the double purpose of road, and of wall to retain the waters of the inundation till they have deposited the fertilising soil over the surface of the fields. During the inundation, these dykes are the only means of travelling, except by boat on the Nile, which may be called the main road throughout the country. This view of Gizeh is taken from the foot of the pyramid in the desert looking towards the east.

Herodotus informs us that during the summer months there is a constant wind blowing from the north; and you will see, on closer inspection of the photograph, all the date-trees inclining to the right, agitated by the Etesian wind which rushes up the valley of the Nile from the Mediterranean Sea to temper the heated air of the desert plains, which form the boundary of Egypt to the east and west. There is not a single stone in the village wall or in any of the huts that has been honestly cut out of the quarry, but every one has been stolen out of the ancient tombs in the neighbourhood.

J. B.

Note.—The palm-trees, in sight, are the date palm of Lower Egypt, with one unbranched stem. The Doum palm of Upper Egypt has branches.

S. S.

PLATE VI.

The Quarries of Toura, and Pyramids.

IN this one little picture we have brought together the most ancient monuments of civilized man now existing on the face of the globe and the most recent invention; for, in the distance, are the pyramids of Gizeh, and in the plain, in the foreground, may be seen the poles of the telegraph wires.

From these quarries, it is said, the stone which forms the casing of the two great pyramids was taken, and in one of the excavations may be seen an ancient carving representing the mode of moving blocks of stone from the quarry. On the roof of the houses of the military establishment at Toura are many perfect samples of the contrivance for catching the north wind, which, with the position of the Pyramids, mark the cardinal points in this picture, and declare the time at which this view was taken to be the afternoon.

The dark background to the rather conspicuous Turkish house, provided with two Malakef, is formed by some fine specimens of the sycamore fig-tree. A small island to the right, about a mile in length, intercepts the view of the main stream between it and the Pyramids; but farther in and to the left is the smaller stream, called the Bahr Usuf. This stream takes its departure from the Nile in the Hermopolite nome about 130 miles south of this spot, and after supplying anciently the artificial lake, Mœris, maunders close along the margin of the desert, entering the Rosetta branch of the Nile forty miles north of the spot.

J. B.

VI.—THE QUARRIES OF TOURA, AND PYRAMIDS.

NOTE.—This village of Toura the Greek writers have called Troja, or Troy, thus giving us a good example of their unhappy custom of changing such foreign names as sounded new to them into others to which they were more accustomed. In this way they have done much to confuse our knowledge of Egypt. The old city of This or Abou-this they named Abydus, after a city in Asia Minor; the capital of Egypt, Tape, they called Thebæ, after a city in Bœotia; the city of Hanes, Tape-hanes, they called Daphnæ; the city of Hahiroth they called Heroopolis. To add to the confusion, in several of these cases the Greeks invented some tradition to explain how the Greek name got into Egypt.

From the word Ouro, *a king*, with the article prefixed, the quarries seem to have received their present name of Toura, the *royal* quarries.

S. S.

PLATE VII.

Siout, or Lycopolis.

THIS view is from the east; Siout is at some little distance from the margin of the Nile on which the spectator is standing, and is to be reached during the inundation only by that road over the bridge which likewise serves as a wall to retain the water, and give it time to deposit a certain thickness of new earth brought down from the higher lands of Ethiopia. At Gizeh we saw the inundation at its full height. Here already the water has deserted the field to the left of the dyke. At Siout there is a mosque or two of considerable size, and a large public bath built by the son-in-law of the famous Mohammed Defterdar Bey on his return from the conquest of Senaar. All these buildings are made out of the ancient materials found on the spot, and at the ancient tombs in the mountains to the south of the town. Siout is an important town on account of the caravans which arrive there from Dar Foor and Kordofan, and other places from the interior of Africa in that direction.

J. B.

NOTE.—Siout in the old Egyptian language is a dog, wolf, or jackal, and hence the name of this city, which the Greeks called Lycopolis, the city of the wolf.

S. S.

PLATE VIII.

Temple of Dendera.

THESE capitals form part of a small temple, the least important of the three temples of Dendera.

This capital is of the composite order, a cluster of full-blown heads of the papyrus plant; between each is a sample of the same plant less expanded, and again between each a bud. The abacus is nearly a cube, on all four sides of which is a grotesque figure. The next capital differs from the first according to the usual Egyptian manner, but it is so nearly buried that any description would be unintelligible. On the wall of the cella an Arab sailor has drawn some boats.

J. B.

NOTE.—The names upon this temple are Trajan, Hadrian, and Antoninus Pius, in whose reigns it was built.

The dwarf figure with a large head sculptured on the square block above the capital, has been sometimes called the wicked god Typhon, who put Osiris to death. But it has a better claim to be thought the pigmy Pthah, a god particularly worshipped at Memphis. Fig. 6. is from a statue of this god in the British Museum. He is described by Herodotus, who visited his temple at Memphis; but he is never found on the older Theban temples, nor in any part of the country before the fall of the Theban power. He was the father of the Cabeiri, a class of pigmy gods, whose employment it was to torture the wicked with swords, snakes, lizards, and serpents.

Fig. 6.

VIII.—TEMPLE OF DENDERA.

Fig. 7 is from a mummy case in the British Museum, which shows us this pigmy Pthah with his children, the Cabeiri, and the lake of fire into which they would throw the wicked.

Fig. 7.

Typhon, on the other hand, who killed Osiris, is represented as a hippopotamus, sometimes walking on his hind legs, and often standing before the judge Osiris demanding that the deceased man should be punished.

S. S.

PLATE IX.

Errebeh—Thebes.

The circular inclosures, made of mud and broken jars, are the rooms or huts open to the sky in which the labourers sleep. In the jars they keep water, butter, cheese, bread, and food of all sorts. This is the first village which the traveller enters when he arrives at Thebes, and lands on the western bank. The jars are made at a place ten miles farther north, called Ballas. From Ballas they are sent down the river for sale in the Delta. They are tied together by sticks, and thus form a raft, on which the owners float down the Nile during the time of the inundation. They are the water jars of all Egypt.

When those picturesque shaped jars called Balas have lost their porosity or a handle, or are cracked and can no longer be used for stowing away dry provisions, they are used in the construction of the mud wall of the miserable hut in which the fellah or peasant of Upper Egypt lives. These vessels take their name from the place where they are made, which is about ten or twelve miles north of Thebes and on the western bank of the Nile. The Balas is the jar in which the women of Egypt fetch water from the river or well, and which they carry with so much profit and grace. The weight of the empty vessel is from 8 to 10 oka, that is, from 22 to $25\frac{1}{2}$ pounds, and when full from 30 to 42 oka, that is, from 76 pounds to 107 pounds and a half. Groups of women are to be seen on the banks of the river in the early morning filling their vessels and assisting each other to lift them on to their heads, which are provided with a padded ring of five or six inches diameter. By this contrivance the great weight which otherwise would bear on a single point is distributed, and the load is carried much to the strengthening of the spine and improvement of the figure. Various other forms of jars are to be seen in this view. One in the wall of the foreground, unlike the Balas, is

IX.—ERREBEK—THEBES.

of red earth, and has no handle, but a knob or button. This contrivance is for fastening it to the chaplet of jars that is attached to the water wheel for scooping up the water which during the low Nile is some distance below the field to be irrigated.

This village is situated among the ruins of the approaches to the temple, and now almost deserted, because of its proximity to the river; the inhabitants being more exposed to sudden incursions made on them by the governor of the province for taxes or unrequited labour in the canals at the season of the inundation. Farther inland there is a greater security of person and property, for the intricacies of the tombs still serve as the refuge of the persecuted and the residence of the disaffected, as they did in the time of Athanasius.

J. B.

Note.—Errebek, or without the Arabic article, Rebek, is one of the old names for Thebes, though it is now given to one only of the villages which stand within the limits of that once great city. From the Coptic words ra, *the sun*, and baki, *city*, we have ra-baki, *the city of the sun*, as Thebes was once called. The original city of Thebes was wholly on the eastern side of the Nile: it was only when it became the capital of all Egypt that the buildings stretched over this western bank.

S. S.

PLATE X.

The Temple of Errebek—Thebes.

THE blocks of stone are the ruined gateway and sphinxes which formed the approach to this temple, of which we see part of the portico, which once had a row of ten columns in front. Behind are seen the western hills in which were buried the Theban kings and queens.

J. B.

NOTE.—Fig. 8 is a ground plan of this temple, and it well explains the larger number of the Egyptian temples. The stranger enters the first courtyard through a doorway between two large towers. He crosses this courtyard between a row of sphinxes, and then enters the second courtyard between two other towers of the same size. This court he also crosses between a row of sphinxes. He is then in front of the portico, and is at liberty to witness the sacrificial ceremonies which take place beneath it. But he is not at liberty to enter the small and mostly dark rooms beyond. These are entered by the priests alone. This temple was at the same time of some strength against any engineering skill that could then be brought against it. Soldiers placed upon the towers of the gateway would by darts and arrows easily forbid an entrance.

S. S.

PLATE XI.

The Temple of Erпebek—Portico.

Each column in this portico is in imitation of a cluster of eight papyrus stalks, of which the buds form the capital. Beneath the buds the stalks are tied about by bands, which are required to form the bundle of the real rushes into a solid post. This view shows the centre intercolumniation, as may be seen by looking at Plate 10. It is wider than the others, and hence the architrave stone has cracked with its great length. Behind is seen the entrance into the back part of the temple.

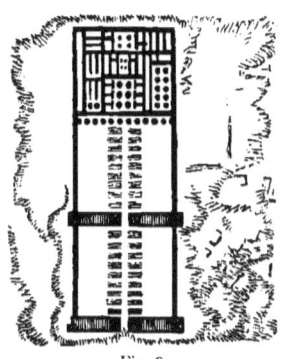

Fig. 8.

Fig. 8. is a plan of this temple.

J. B.

Note.—This temple was built by Oimenepthah I., whose name (fig. 9) often appears on it. But it was finished by his son, Rameses II.

On the abacus, or square stone above the papyrus-formed capital, is the name of the great king who finished this, and built so many of the temples of Egypt, "The Son of the sun, Amunmai Rameses." His titles are again written on the architrave or slab which passes from column to

Fig. 9.

XI.—THE TEMPLE OF ERREBEK—PORTICO.

column. This long inscription is to be read in both directions, beginning in the middle, and in each half the reader meets the faces of the animals: "The king, the brave, beloved by Amun, sole lord of the diadem, lord of Egypt and of the foreign countries." The eagle-and-ball is the well-known word Pha-roah, *the king*.

Fig. 10.

Fig. 10 is this king's name in full, from another inscription. Its two ovals are translated for us by Hermapion, "Whom the Sun approved," and "Whom Ammon loves, and the Sun has tried."

Rameses II. was the greatest of the Theban kings. He lived about B.C. 1170. He reigned over Upper and Lower Egypt and Ethiopia. He marched his conquering armies, through Palestine, to the Euphrates and the Black Sea. Lest we should have any doubt about the historian's account of his wars, he has left his names and titles carved on the face of the rock at Beyroot in Syria. We must suppose that this invasion of Palestine by the Egyptians overthrew the power of the Philistines, and helped the Israelites to the possession of that portion of the Promised Land.

S. S.

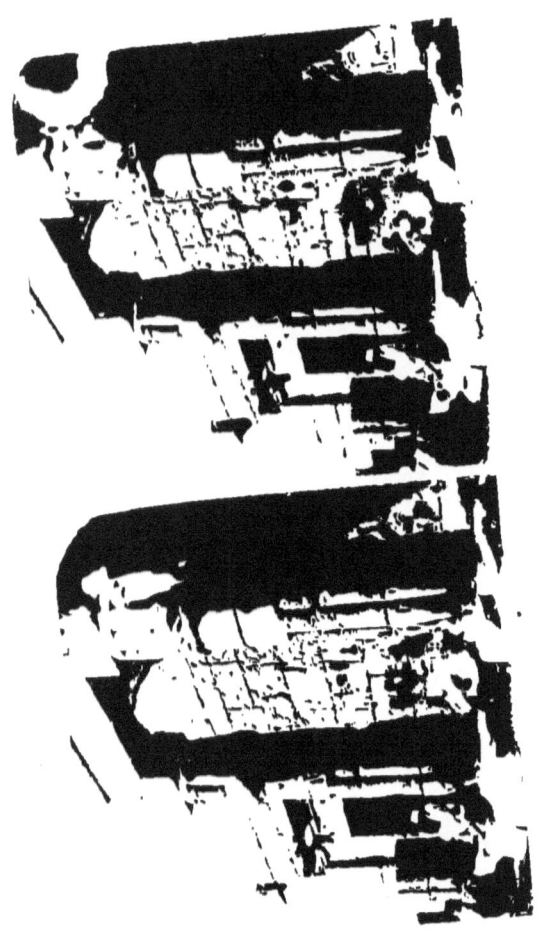

PLATE XII.

The Temple of Errebek—Entrance to Sanctuary.

SCULPTURED on the wall may be seen a row of men, each a Nile-god, carrying three water-jars, and birds and fruits, productions of the river. Above these is a row of priests, carrying on their shoulders the sacred barge.

J. B.

The doorway here seen, beyond the ruined portico, is the entrance to the sanctuary of the temple of Errebek, where the priests, or rather some of them, lived in religious seclusion as monks. It was from these Egyptian priests that the Christians, many centuries afterwards, borrowed their monastic institutions. Other priests came abroad among the people, and filled many of the high offices of state.

S. S.

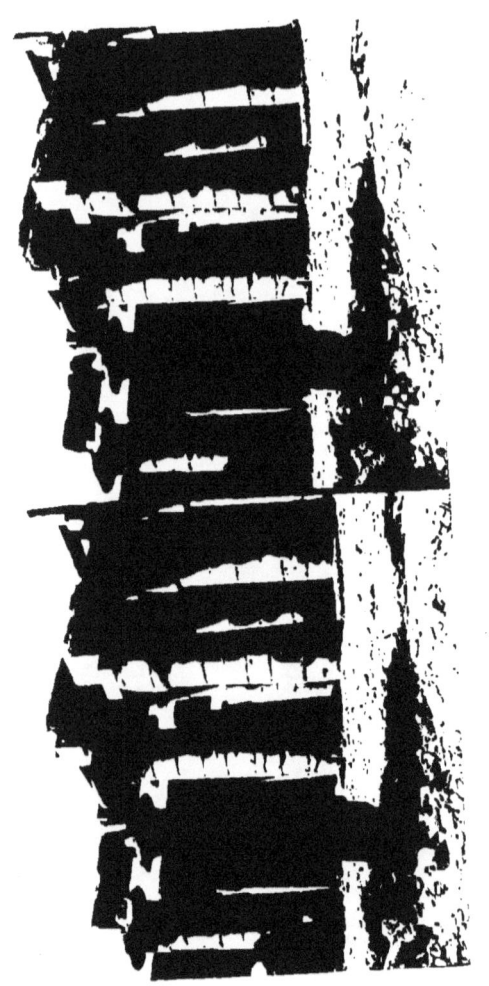

PLATE XIII.

The Memnonium—Thebes.

The centre avenue of columns which support the higher part of the hall, represent the fully expanded flower of the papyrus; and those which support the lower roof, the single stalk and single bud of the same plant. A glance at the plan (see Fig. 11), will explain the arrangement of this hall, and of the whole of the building.

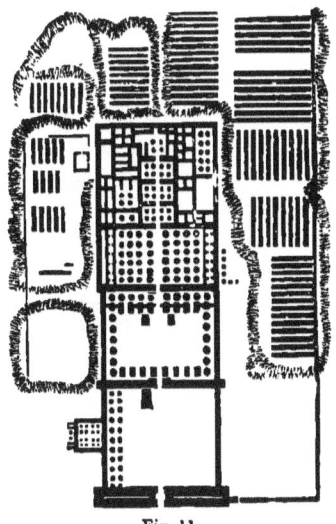

Fig. 11.

It will be observed, that both these orders of columns gradually increase downwards till within about one-sixth of the height from the base,

XIII.—THE MEMNONIUM—THEBES.

when they begin to diminish in diameter, just as the natural plant does when it is enveloped in those close-fitting leaves. And here, too, the likeness is kept up by those curved sculptured lines representing the fibrous structure of the leaves at the base of the natural plant. (See fig. 12.)

Fig. 12.

To return to the capital: The slender separate filaments of the head of the papyrus are sufficiently intimated by those recurring blue lines between the ovals, springing as they do from behind the leaves at the base of the capital, which represent those at the base of the filaments in the natural plant. The other decorative lines are not belonging to the likeness it is intended to bear to the plant, but, apparently, to certain adornments which were attached to the earlier temples, consisting of strips of linen, of red and blue, bound round the bundles of papyrus of which, probably, the primitive shrines were constructed. The ends of these bands are represented as hanging down on the shafts of the columns, representing the papyrus bud. Below these decorations are sculptures— better seen in Plate 14.

In the immediate foreground stands up a block of black granite, which formed the door-post of the entrance to an avenue of the minor columns of this hall. On it is sculptured, in deep incavo-rilievo, a figure of the king walking into the temple. On his head is engraved, in large characters, his name and titles; and on the side some poor Arab boatman has scribbled, in white chalk, the words Ali Altolah, probably his name.

Many of the roof-stones of the central avenue are still in their places.

J. B.

NOTE.—This temple was called by the Egyptians the Miamun-ei, or House of King Miamun; and the Greek travellers, following their usual custom, changed the Egyptian name Miamun into the Greek name Memnon, and named it the Memnonium. On the ceiling is sculptured a table of the

XIII.—THE MEMNONIUM—THEBES.

months or almanac, connecting the civil year with the natural year, which, if made with scientific accuracy, would fix the date of Rameses II., in whose reign it was sculptured. But it shows its own want of accuracy, and does not fix its date in any way that we can at all rely upon.

The Egyptian civil year contained twelve months of thirty days each and five days over, or 365 days; beginning on the day when the dog-star was seen to rise heliacally at daybreak. But, for want of a leap-year the civil new year's day came round one day too fast in every four years. In four times 365 years, the civil new year's day made a complete revolution of the natural year. This period of time was called a Sothic period. One Sothic period began in B.C. 1321, and the next in A.D. 138. In these years, the civil new year's day fell on our 16th July. But the day when the dog-star was seen to rise heliacally varied with the weather and the eyesight of the observer. It was uncertain, to the extent of eight or nine days; and hence the observed beginning of a Sothic period was uncertain to the extent of thirty-six years. Here is our first reason for distrust. Now this almanac on the ceiling of the Memnonium declares, that the civil new year's day fell upon the day of the dog-star's rising heliacally, and also upon the day of the summer solstice; but both of these cannot be strictly true. The new year's day fell upon the true day of the dog-star's rising in the year B.C. 1321; it fell upon the day of the solstice in the year B.C. 1217. Here is our second reason for distrust. Moreover, the almanac does not mention the five extra days of the year; and it divides the year, not by the equinoxes, which give the more accurate division, but in the less exact way by the solstices. Here are other reasons for distrust. Hence it must not be quoted as giving us an exact date for the reign of Rameses II., who made it. All that can be said of it is, that it was made within one or two centuries after the year B.C. 1217—before the difference between the civil new year's day and the day of the solstice had become so great as to be apparent to unscientific eyes. We have other reasons for thinking that Rameses II., who made it, began to reign about the year B.C. 1170.

This temple, which was called by the Egyptians the Miamun-ei, or *House of King Miamun*, was called by Diodorus, the historian, the tomb of Osymandyas—a name which is not much amiss; as, though Rameses II.

XIII.—THE MEMNONIUM—THEBES.

finished it, it was probably begun by his father, whose name the Greeks may have so pronounced. Fig. 9 is the name of the father, and if we give to the sitting figure of Osiris the force of Osi, the second oval becomes Osimenpthah, as he is called by Diodorus. If we give to that character the force of O, it may be read Oimenepthah. Again, if we follow another form in which the name was at first written, with the dog Anubis in the place of Osiris, it becomes Aimenepthah, as this king is called by the historian Manetho.

S. S.

The starry vault of heaven.

PLATE XIV.

The Memnonium—Rear View of the Columns.

THIS view being a nearer view of the columns of the centre avenue, the significant decoration engraved on the surface of them can be more easily discerned. On the column to the right, just below the five bands which encircle the neck of the column, may be distinctly seen the ovals surmounted by the disk of the sun, and guarded by the Uræus or sacred cobra, containing the characters of the name of Rameses the Second (see fig. 10). Below this circle of ovals containing the royal names, is an incised picture of the king attended by his standard-bearer, making offerings to the divinities of the temple. This picture occupies that half of the column which is turned towards the great avenue; the other half has no decoration till just below the band which encircles the shaft at its greatest diameter, where is the king's name again, surmounted by a disk and guarded by sacred asps. This device occurs between each leaf at the base of the shaft, but faintly discernible; and under each oval is an elegant combination of lines. Lying at the base of the nearest column is the pedestal of a statue of the king, as the inscription on it informs us; and representing, as may be presumed, the king walking into the centre avenue. The bases of all these columns are covered with the rubbish of ages, but they have been dug out and measured, and are faithfully represented in the little wood-cut (fig. 13). This part of the temple served as a Christian church in the time of Athanasius; and, in more recent times, was taken possession of

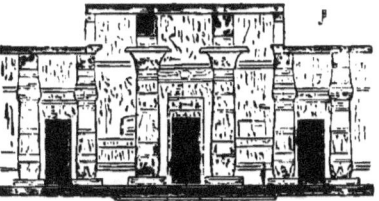

Fig. 13.

XIV.—THE MEMNONIUM—NEAR VIEW OF THE COLUMNS.

by a man of wealth among the Arabs, from whom it acquired and retains to this day among the natives the name of Kuser Degaghe, or the Castle of Degaghe. The smaller chambers behind the hall of columns were occupied by the female members of his family; and he himself, with his sons and large flocks, was wont to repose during the heat of the day beneath the shadow of the columns of the hall. Some descendants of this man were living in Goorna thirty years ago.

J. B.

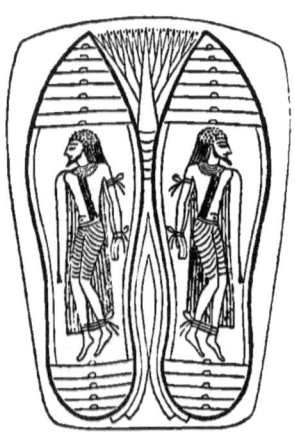

The foot of a mummy case, representing the enemies of the deceased under the soles of his feet.

PLATE XV.

Osiride Columns of the Memnonium.

THIS is a view taken from the second court, looking westward into the centre avenue. From this court Belzoni took the granite head, called by him "the young Memnon," now in the British Museum and of which we give a wood-cut (see fig. 14). It belonged to a seated figure, known since to represent Rameses II. that sat with his back close to those two Caryatid figures standing against the square piers (see Plan, fig. 11). Immediately in the foreground, to the left, is a granite block, the fragment of the companion figure to that of Belzoni, which sat on the other side of the principal entrance from this court to the Hall of Columns. The remains of a dwarf wall, stretching from pier to pier, is still to be seen against the side of the pier of the figure to the right; for beyond this court, it would seem, the Egyptian public was not admitted. The three gates which gave entrance to the portico, the roof of which was supported by the Caryatid figures, were approached by a flight of steps, and the Arab boy sits on the inclined plane which is the margin of the steps of the centre entrance. The piece of wall on the left is that of the Hall of Columns; and this face of it is adorned with a representation of the king making offering to all the divinities of the temple, one of whom, the Theban Pthah or Khonso, is seen seated with the solar disk over his head. The large hieroglyphics behind this figure are those on the left-hand jamb of the central entrance to the Hall of Columns (see fig. 13). The other face of this wall is occupied by

Fig. 14.

XV.—OSIRIDE COLUMNS OF THE MEMNONIUM.

a large historical picture, of great interest, representing the besieging of a city built on a rocky eminence. The Egyptians are scaling the walls, in which operation they are led on by a son of the king; while the king himself, of gigantic proportions, puts to flight the entire army. No man escapes the royal shaft, not even he on horseback designed to show the utter defeat and consternation of the enemy; for, it would appear from these genuine records, that neither the Egyptians, nor the nations bordering on Egypt to the north, had, at the time to which this picture refers, any cavalry, properly so called. And it may, therefore, be matter of discussion whether the word for *horsemen*, in Exodus xiv. 9, should not be understood to mean, "the warrior in the chariot" or the charioteer. There is a copy of this picture in the Crystal Palace.

The court from which this view is taken is surrounded by a portico, of which the roof on two sides is supported by columns, while at the two ends it is supported by three Caryatid figures (see Plan,) representing the king, in the form of Osiris, as supreme judge. He holds in his right hand the crook and in his left the flail, as guide of the good and punisher of the wicked. Down the front of this mummy-form figure is a line of hieroglyphics, in which may be read the names of Rameses II.

J. B.

Note.—These are the columns mentioned by Diodorus as upholding the roof in one of the courts of the Memnonium. The figures, he says, were fifteen cubits high: each figure holds the whip and crosier, the two sceptres of the god Osiris. They are portraits of the king: the sceptres tell us, that he is upon death changed into the character of that god. Agreeably to this, those hieroglyphical inscriptions which mention a dead man, usually give him the title of Osiris; which we must translate as Osiris-like, or acquitted by the judge Osiris.

The dwarf wall which, in this temple, is introduced between the columns, marks an interesting change in their religious feelings since the Temple of Errebek was built, in the last reign. In that temple, the laity in the court-yard could see what took place among the priests under the

XV.—OSIRIDE COLUMNS OF THE MEMNONIUM.

portico; but in this newer temple their profane eyes are shut out from the sight of sacred rites, to which the priests only were admitted. Henceforth all Egyptian temples are built with these dwarf walls or screens against the vulgar, till they were removed, ten centuries later, in the reigns of the Ptolemies. The remains of the wall may be seen between the two Osiris-like figures, and reached up to about the knee.

The god Khonso, on the left-hand wall, is the son of Ammon Ra and of the goddess Athor, and with them he is the third person in the Theban Trinity.

S. S.

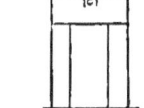

Doorway to a tomb or temple.

PLATE XVI.

The fallen Colossus of the Memnonium.

THIS view is taken from the same court as the last, but looking to the north. And here we see, in the sloping line of mountains which forms the background, the reason for the name which this district of Thebes has acquired from the Arab inhabitants : it is the spur or foot of the limestone hills which gives to the stream that projection to the east desert, forming an angle— Goorna or Kurna, or *horn*—behind which the district is, as it were, shut in. It was in marching over this spur that the French army, after leaving Dendera, first got sight of the plain of Thebes. From the elevated ground the monuments are spread out as in a map, and the whole army was awed at the scene which then suddenly opened upon it. As before-mentioned, the roof of the portico of two sides of this court was supported by columns, and the two ends by Caryatides. The north wall of the court has entirely disappeared, and only two columns are left of the portico ; but we have all the four Caryatid figures at the opposite end : they support the roof-stones that stretch from the wall to the piers. The pier of the nearest Caryatid is divided into three compartments; in the uppermost is the king on his knees, making an offering to Pthah. In the next, the king is seen in long sacerdotal robes, making offering to Horus. And in the lower compartment he is walking into the temple, and met and welcomed at the entrance by Amun, the chief divinity of Thebes. On this pier, which is that on the north side of the gate, the king wears the crown of Lower Egypt ; but on the other, if it existed, we should see him wearing the crown of Upper Egypt. On the wall behind the pier is a large historical incised picture, representing the besieging of a city surrounded by water. The Egyptian king, here again a giant, is driving the enemy into a large river which encircles a fortified city. Other streams intersect the picture, by the side of which the Egyptian army

XVI.—THE FALLEN COLOSSUS OF THE MEMNONIUM.

is advancing in chariots *drawn by two horses*, in which are three persons : the warrior, his shield-bearer, and charioteer. There is no Egyptian on horseback, and only one or two of the enemy, who are in rapid flight, yet wounded, for a horse is but a vain thing to save a man who contends with the Egyptian king! All the chariots of the enemy are upset; and the chosen captains of the enemy, known by their long and embroidered garments and inscriptions over them, are drowned in the river, "sunk into the bottom as a stone," for no representation can express more faithfully the phraseology of the Bible. On the other shore are some that have escaped the water, though not the royal shaft, being helped out by their friends. Hard by the gate of the city, the enemy is drawn up in battle array. There is a great deal of colour left on this picture. Above is a procession of priests carrying the statues of the kings, before each his name, and among them that of Menes.

The ceiling of this portico still retains the blue paint and yellow stain mentioned by Diodorus. Between each couple of roof-stones are two square perforations, which give light and air; yet hardly for this alone can these holes be contrived, for they are not more than four inches square— but, probably, for the insertion of square poles on which to extend an awning on the roof for sleeping under.

In the foreground is lying, on its back, the largest isolated statue in the world. It is cut out of a block of granite as big as that on which the statue of Peter the Great is standing at St. Petersburg. The name of the author of this work has been preserved to us in the account which Diodorus has given of this temple. When or by whom this masterpiece of ancient art was thrown down off its pedestal, is unknown. In its fall it has broken from the seat, and, again, across the waist. The French architects estimated its weight at two millions of pounds. This statue was placed in the first court, on the left hand of the entrance to the second. An historical incised picture of the same event as this described, occupies the entire surface of the propylon. On the left wing is the king giving audience in his camp. On the right, the battle and siege of the same fortified place surrounded by water. Each picture is not less than one hundred feet long, and was fifty feet high. The whole front of this propylon is a ruin.

During the inundation, the Nile reaches to the front of this propylon:

XVI.—THE FALLEN COLOSSUS OF THE MEMNONIUM.

and at that season of the year it is not unusual to find snakes, and among them the serpent called the Uræus, which the kings of Egypt wear in their crowns, taking refuge from the water. This snake inflates its neck and resembles in outward appearance that to which the Spanish Americans gave the name of Cobra capello, which in that country is a deadly reptile, but in Egypt, some men of science assert, it is not venomous. Some of these serpents measure six feet in length; and it is no unusual thing to see a serpent-charmer in the streets of Cairo, making one of this size dance with his head and neck erect, to the sound of a pipe and drum.

The whole of this structure is of sandstone except the two minor entrances to the hall of columns and the isolated sculptures, which are of granite. Surrounding this ruin are some long vaults built of unburnt bricks, having the name of Rameses II. stamped on them.

The figure of Amun on the door-post of the principal entrance has the eyelid and eyebrow pierced out for the purpose of inserting metal or other material. This may possibly have been done at some much later period.

J. B.

Note.—The chariots in the battle-scene described by Mr. Bonomi are of high interest to the biblical scholar, containing as they do three men in each: one to drive, one to guard with a shield, and one to strike with a spear. We read, in Exodus xiv. 7, that when the chariots of Egypt pursued the Israelites, who were leaving Egypt under the guidance of Moses, there were three Egyptians in each chariot. This curious piece of information is unhappily lost to us in the Authorized English Version, which simply says that "there were captains over every one of them."

S. S.

PLATE XVII.

Foundations of the Temple near Dayr-el-Bahree, Thebes.

This view is taken from the east looking directly west towards the perpendicular rocks which separate this valley of the Assasseef from the valley of the Biban el Moluk.

In the immediate foreground is one of those square areas of excavation in the fine limestone rock of this district, leading to chambers and mummy-pits, that have long since been sacked and destroyed by fire and water, and so incumbered with rubbish that they are little known to modern explorers. Most of the tombs in this part of the valley have for years served the Arab population of Gournou and its neighbourhood as hiding-places from Turkish despotism; the difficulty of access, their vastness and intricacy, making them convenient places of refuge for the people and their cattle, and the dry mummy-pits safe places for corn. All the tombs in this district partake more or less of this character of intricacy and darkness by contrast from the surrounding debris of white limestone; and hence probably the name of the place, which is derived from the Arabic word *assat*, to grope and feel one's way as a blind man. A little farther on are two brick propylons in walls twenty feet thick, with well-built arches—particularly the farther one, which has rows of bricks forming the arch. In this thick high wall was probably a staircase, and small chambers for the priests or guardians of the tombs. Behind it is a large court surrounded by a high and thick brick wall, and a flight of steps let down to the square excavation, with entrances to chambers excavated in the rock on three sides of the square.

In this same valley, only a stone's throw from the more perfect gateway,

XVII.—FOUNDATIONS OF THE TEMPLE NEAR DAYR-EL-BAHREE.

is one of these tombs, where chambers are more accessible than this one. You enter by an arch-formed excavation in the rock, the ceiling of which has been elaborately painted. This porch leads into a large chamber whose ceiling is supported by twelve piers. From this chamber you descend by steps to another which leads into several others on the same level, filled with curious sculptures, and from these again you descend to another set of apartments. This tomb is one of the most remarkable in Thebes; its sculptures are in the style of those of the time of Psammetichus I.

Besides the tombs in this valley, there are many crude brick constructions of great interest; one very large inclosure called Dayr sa Callio, so-called from having been adopted as a residence by one of the first Egyptian explorers, Monsieur Calliaud. The walls of this structure on the outside are curiously panelled in grooves and squares, not unlike the tombs which surround the great pyramid of Gizeh. There are also some pyramidal structures with some oven-shaped cavities; perhaps the places where the different processes of mummification were carried on. Indeed the whole district wears a singular appearance, and the tombs some peculiar features.

J. B.

PLATE XVIII.

Buildings and Rocks near Dayr-el-Bahree.

DAYR EL BAHREE, or the Northern Convent, so called from that brick structure with a row of windows, and the tower with sloping walls immediately under the perpendicular cliffs. This view is taken from what seems formerly to have been a road up to the ancient temple, which stood on the site of the convent; for it lies between little mounds of limestone, which were so many sphinxes. Behind the brick building are some chambers of the age of Thothmes cut in rock, and an ancient granite gateway. It was believed that these chambers led to others that opened into the valley of the tombs of the kings, called the Biban el Moluk, close by the tomb of Osiris or Oimenephthah I., discovered by Belzoni, a distance of about 1,000 feet from the face of those magnificent cliffs so admirably defined in the photograph. Near this spot, to the right, is a path leading over these rocks into the valley of the tombs of the kings. In the same valley of this Dayr or convent, is a large excavated tomb, before the entrance to which are some extensive brick walls, which are certainly those of a Christian building, made out of ancient materials; for on the wall of the tomb, which had been plastered for the purpose, are the remains of an inscription beginning, "I, Athanasius, bishop of Alexandria." A few other words, perhaps, might be picked up among the fragments of the plaster on which it was written, now fallen on the ground. It is very probable this inscription has not been any more perfect than it now is since first intelligent modern travellers have visited this interesting locality, or we should have had copies of it.

J. B.

PLATE XIX.

The Plain of Thebes, with New Excavations.

In going from the Assasseef to Medinet-Habou, the next important building to the Memnonium, on this side the river, and keeping on the high ground among the tombs, you come to the Ptolemaic temple called Dayr el Medineh. It obtained this name, probably, from having become the residence of religious persons connected with the Christian establishments of Medinet-Habou, when those ruined houses on and about the temple of Rameses III. were inhabited, and formed a considerable district of Christian Thebes, during the first four centuries of our era. From the high ground behind this temple, and looking directly east, you have the view of the plains of Thebes exhibited in this photograph. In the extreme distance are the mountains of the desert between the Red Sea and the Nile, out of which emeralds and gold were dug. Bearing slightly to the north, or travelling from the ruin in the foreground right over the arches of the Memnonium and crossing the Nile, where that white latine sail appears, you would arrive at the quarries of porphyry, verd antique, and breccia, worked by the Romans; and, at last, at the port of Cosseir on the Red Sea. The dark tint below the mountains to the edge of the desert, on this side the river, shows the extent of the inundation, or the cultivatable land, in fact, the width of Egypt at this particular part. That little square projection in the dark tint just over the Memnonium, is the propylon of the temple of Karnak, exactly three miles from the spot from whence this view is taken. Egypt, then, in the neighbourhood of its great capital, Amun No, is not more than fifteen miles wide, for the desert is no more Egypt than is the Red Sea or the Mediterranean. Looking at the vastness of the ruins, one wonders whence a city, so situated, could have derived its supplies and could have become so celebrated, both in sacred and profane history; or how

XIX.—THE PLAIN OF THEBES, WITH NEW EXCAVATIONS.

it could have been compared to Nineveh, as we read in Nahum, if one did not, at the same time, take into consideration that " Ethiopia and Egypt were her strength, and it was infinite;" for the Nile, serving as a road, brought the men and produce of those regions, which were unknown and, so to speak, infinite. " Put and Lubim were thy helpers." That is to say, all that region of Africa, along the coast of the Mediterranean to the west of Egypt, called Libya by the Greeks, was also tributary to Egypt ; probably those nations signified in the inscriptions by nine bows, and which the statues of Rameses have under their feet (see fig. 15), embodying the metaphor so commonly used in the Bible to signify absolute dominion.

Fig. 15.

On the edge of the desert, on this side the river, may be clearly seen the propylon of the Memnonium, the fallen Colossus, the columns of the Hall of Assembly, and the long brick arches which range with the stone building. Still nearer, the crude brick wall that surrounds the Dayr; and, lastly, the arch built up against the stone wall of the temple. This arch is of the same construction as those about the Memnonium, which are built of bricks stamped with the name of Rameses II., and recently shown by Mr. Falkener to be of a construction peculiar to ancient Egypt.

Within this temple, below the pavement of the vestibule, was found, in a subterranean chamber, the wig of false hair now in the British Museum. The temple was built by Ptolemy Philopator, and carried on by some of his successors. The construction, like all those temples of the Ptolemies, is excellent ; and there are some peculiarities in design which make this example interesting to the architect. Pilasters, with the head of Athor, support an architrave with columns of the composite order, to which they are joined by the usual intercolumnar wall. There is also a decorated window giving light to a staircase leading to the roof.

J. B.

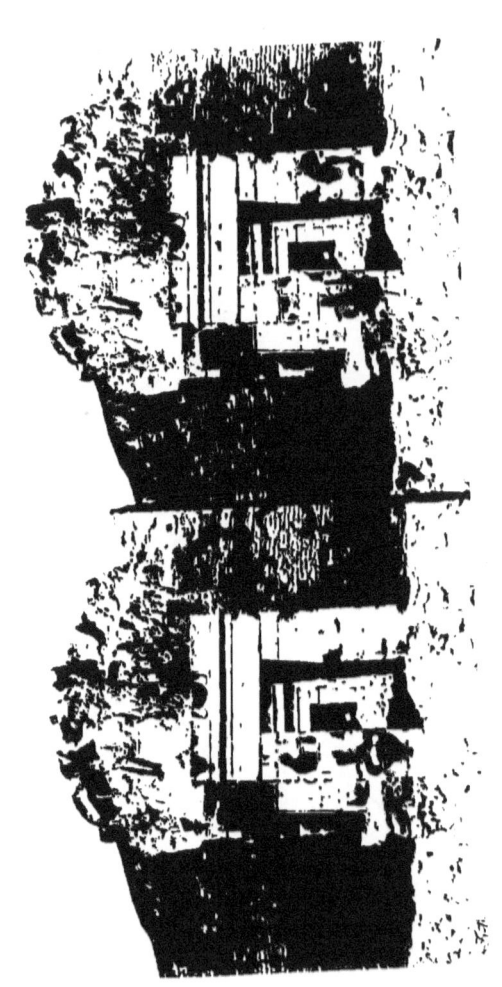

PLATE XX.

The Temple near Dayr-el-Medineh.

THE sculptures on this pylon or gateway are of the third century before our era. The stones which formed the upper part of the curvetto, and consequently the upper half of the winged disk, with the heads of the asps, have fallen down. Enough, however, remains to show that it has been highly decorated with those graceful channels which belong to this constant feature of Egyptain architecture. The next stone, out of which is carved the head or torus, is one single block, stretching across and resting on the architrave stone, which also of necessity is one single block, and of a sufficient thickness to insure its capability of supporting the weight of the superstructure; for the stones above the architrave do not extend all across, but serve as a parapet wall for the passage over the gate, from the staircase which would have been constructed in the thickness of the wall on either side of the gate. The torus has its appropriate enrichment, viz. the flat band, as it were, twisted round it in one oblique and two straight turns. The sculptures on the architrave stone are less distinct than those on the door jambs. Four times on each jamb Ptolemy Philopator is making offering to so many of the divinities of Egypt, and each accompanied by a goddess.

In the interior of the gate, and on the left-hand side, is engraved a figure of Christ, in front view and in a seated position. This figure, which no doubt is the work of the early Christians, who had converted the building into a Christian place of worship, has scarcely ever been noticed, and never that we are aware of been drawn. No doubt other indications would be found of the occupation of this building by the early Christians, even before the time of that Greek inscription of Athanasius, already mentioned, if diligent search

XX.—THE TEMPLE NEAR DAYR-EL-MEDINEH.

were made, particularly among the brick ruins now incumbering this beautiful structure.

On the wall of one of the smaller chambers at the back is the name of Augustus Cæsar.—*See* WILKINSON'S *Thebes.*

J. B.

NOTE.—Over the doorway is the figure of the winged sun, with an asp, or sacred snake, on each side of it. This was the figure of the god Amun-ra; and by the wings the Egyptian meant to express the same figurative thought as the Hebrew Psalmist, who says of the Almighty, that men put their trust under the shadow of His wings.

The inscription in honour of the great Athanasius, in this and other places in the western half of Thebes, is a proof that the spot was not occupied as a military station by the Greek troops. Athanasius was the popular bishop with the native Egyptians, while his Arian rival George was the bishop of the Greeks living in the country. Hence George had churches built to his honour in those few places where the Greek soldiers were numerous; while in the larger places, such as Alexandria and Thebes, the churches were often dedicated to Athanasius.

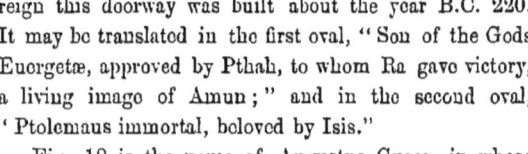

Fig. 17.

Fig. 18.

Fig 17 is the name of Ptolemy Philopator, in whose reign this doorway was built about the year B.C. 220. It may be translated in the first oval, "Son of the Gods Euergetæ, approved by Pthah, to whom Ra gave victory, a living image of Amun;" and in the second oval, "Ptolemaus immortal, beloved by Isis."

Fig. 18 is the name of Augustus Cæsar, in whose reign some of the chambers at the back were added. It may be read "Autocrator Caisaros immortal, beloved by Pthah and Isis."

S. S.

PLATE XXI.

The Two Colossal Statues of Memnon—Thebes.

THIS is a view of the two statues in the plain of Goorna. To nothing but the colossal dimensions of the work and the excessive hardness of the material, is to be attributed any remains of these monuments of ancient art and engineering science. Every conceivable effort has been made by fanatic ignorance to destroy these historical landmarks. Fires have been lit on the laps and on the pedestals of these figures, which have split off large pieces of stone from the front view, and entirely destroyed all trace of the features; yet, here they stand monuments of ancient jugglery and superstition, to which modern science and scholarship has made them bear unequivocal witness.

Our view is taken from the south, looking towards that spur of limestone rock before alluded to, and from which the name of this district of modern Thebes is derived. Both statue and pedestal are made out of blocks of hard red grit-stone, commonly called plum-pudding stone. The nearer statue is of one single block, not less than 38 or 40 feet high. The farther statue was originally of one block; but we are informed by Strabo, who visited this spot about twenty or twenty-five years before our era, that the upper part of one had been thrown down by an earthquake. It appears from his account that he came to this spot in company with Ælius Gallus, and numerous friends, and soldiers, to hear the musical sounds which this broken statue was said to give out at sunrise; for it was supposed that it represented Memnon, the son of Aurora, who was killed in the Trojan war.

The testimony of one of these witnesses bears most interestingly on the greatest literary discoveries of modern times, namely, the discovery of the phonetic value of certain hieroglyphics; for he declares that he heard the " statue which the Greeks call Memnon, and the Egyptians call

XXI.—THE TWO COLOSSAL STATUES OF MEMNON—THEBES.

Amunoph, give out sounds." Among those curious and intelligently formed signs, engraved with such artistic precision in the hard stone of which the statue is made, are the characters composing the name of the Egyptian monarch Amunothph III. They are contained in the oval to the left of the central division of the ornamental writing on the side of the throne.

Fig. 19.

Two figures of the god Nilus, perhaps signifying Upper and Lower Egypt, or perhaps the eastern and western banks of the Nile, are represented in the act of binding up the stem of the throne of Egypt with a curious knot of water plants. This same device (see fig. 19), with or without the figures of the god, is engraved on the thrones of the statues of both the gods and kings of the country.

The head of the more distant figure of Nilus still retains the stain of the plaster cast made more than thirty years ago; so conservative is the climate of Egypt, and so excellent the photograph, that the erasure and subsequent insertion of the hieroglyphics now contained within the second oval of the king's name can be discerned. Having noticed the fact, we will not detain our readers in this place with the very interesting speculations dependent on that circumstance, but proceed to describe the rest of the work. On each side of the leg of the most colossal figure stands a female figure, one representing the mother, and the other the wife of the king. This view of the group does not permit us to see more than the back of the head, the shoulder, and the arm of one of these figures. The head is a little above the level of the seat, having a modius or crown on it; and the pendent tresses, covering the shoulders, can be distinctly seen by the aid of a magnifying glass in the farther statue. These figures cannot be less than sixteen feet high. In these colossal sitting statues of the Pharaohs, whenever the mother and wife of the monarch are associated, they are always placed, as we see them in this example, with their backs against the throne on each side of the principal figure, while the figure of the son of the king is placed standing between his feet. The constancy of this arrangement forbids us attributing it to the caprice of the artist; it is

XXI.—THE TWO COLOSSAL STATUES OF MEMNON—THEBES.

more probably the embodiment of an ancient idea or custom, from which was likewise derived the metaphor used by Israel while in this very country, to signify perpetuity of legitimate succession; "The sceptre shall not depart from Judah, *nor a lawgiver from between his feet*, until he come to Shiloh."

It cannot be ascertained from Strabo's account of his visits to these statues, or from any of the numerous Greek and Latin inscriptions engraved on the vocal statue, whether the upper part had already been restored, as we now see it. The probability is that it was, and that the wilful injury done to them was the work of the invaders under Cambyses. The great fissure across the massive block of the throne is very like the effect of lightning, which was more probably the cause of the destruction of the upper part than an earthquake; for one cannot conceive why the companion statue should have escaped, or that any part of the Memnonium should have been left standing. It would appear that these statues formed part of an avenue of colossi belonging to a temple situated several hundred paces behind them; and from that ruin ten or twelve feet below the level of the pavement, in a line with the statues, were discovered the two beautiful granite Sphinxes now in St. Petersburg. From the same ruin likewise came those heads in the same stone as the vocal statue of singular features in the British Museum. There is, in fact, a mysterious interest about all the temples and statues bearing the name of Amunothph III. which is far from being exhausted, and to which we shall have occasion to allude as we proceed up the Nile.

J. B.

NOTE.—Of these two statues the most northerly is the musical statue, famed for uttering musical notes at sunrise, when its lips were first saluted by Aurora. The Greeks called it the statue of Memnon, changing the Egyptian name of King Amunothph into Memnon for more easy pronunciation, as they for the same reason changed the name of King Miamun into the same word. Thus they gave this statue of Amunothph III.

XXI.—THE TWO COLOSSAL STATUES OF MEMNON—THEBES.

and one of the temples of Miamun Rameses II. both to the same person, namely to a King Memnon of their own creating.

This priestly trick of the music uttered by the statue at sunrise, must have been practised at a very early time, at least before the time of Hesiod, who, writing about the year B.C. 800, calls Memnon, King of Ethiopia, the son of the goddess Aurora. Ethiopia was at that early time a name given to the Thebaïd; and thus Hesiod gives us a fabulous connection between Amunothph king of Thebes, and Aurora, which seems to spring from the musical notes of this statue at sunrise.

When the Persians, under Cambyses, conquered Egypt in B.C. 523, this northerly statue was already the most important of the two; for they took the trouble, in their zeal to insult the Egyptians, to break this Colossus in half at the waist, and to throw the upper part to the ground, while they left its fellow statue standing and unhurt. It was only when the statue was in this broken state that the music was first heard and described by the Greek travellers. When Strabo, Juvenal, and Pausanias listened to the sounds, the upper half of the statue was still lying on the ground. So it was when the Roman Emperor Hadrian and his wife Sabina visited it. It was either after Hadrian's reign, or late in his reign, that the Romans, to please the Egyptians, set up again the broken pieces of this statue, and left it as we now see it.

Travellers, on reaching a distant point of their journey, or viewing any remarkable object of curiosity, have at all times been fond of carving or scribbling their names on the spot, to boast of their prowess to after-comers; and never had any place been more favoured with memorials of this kind than the musical statue of Amunothph at Thebes. Under the Romans the journey through Upper Egypt was perfectly open and safe; and the legs and feet of this colossal statue are covered with names and inscriptions, in prose and verse, of travellers who visited it at sunrise, during the reigns of Hadrian and the Antonines, to hear its musical notes. From these curious memorials we learn the names of Egyptian prefects, otherwise unknown to history; and from the same we learn that Hadrian visited Egypt a second time, with his queen Sabina, in the fifteenth year of his reign. When the empress first visited the

XXI.—THE TWO COLOSSAL STATUES OF MEMNON—THEBES.

statue, she was disappointed at not hearing the musical sounds; but on her hinting threats of the emperor's displeasure, the priests gratified her curiosity on the following morning.

Fig. 20.

Fig. 20 is the name of King Amunothph III., preceded by the titles Lord of the World and Lord of Battles.

S. S.

PLATE XXII.

The Temple of Medinet-Habou — Thebes.

"AND when he heard say of Tirhakah, King of Ethiopia, Behold he is come out to fight against thee, he sent messengers again unto Hezekiah." 2 Kings, xix. 9.

In the foreground of this view are the gateways and the columns of a small temple built by the Ethiopian king, mentioned in this quotation. In all probability Tirhakah built this little temple on his return from Palestine, when his presence, with an armed force, frightened the boastful Sennacherib into the sending again messengers to Hezekiah to threaten the destruction of Jerusalem, and thereby to extort an excess of tribute, before the King of Ethiopia could arrive to prevent it. The identification of this ruin with the Ethiopian ally of Hezekiah, is no matter of conjecture, but a fact recorded at the time by a sculpture engraved on that wall in the shade cast by the unfinished tower of the Ptolemaic gateway on the right. The hieroglyphics constituting the name of this King of Ethiopia, were first discovered on the walls of a temple in Ethiopia by Lord Prudhoe and Major Felix more than thirty years ago, and since that time the figure of Tirhakah, decapitating a group of Asiatic prisoners, has been brought to light on the wall in front of this temple. The name of that king is written both on this ruin and that of Ethiopia as in the wood-cut in the margin, the second oval containing the letters THRK. (Fig. 21.)

Fig. 21.

Again, it is no matter of conjecture that the unfinished tower, which casts a shade on the front wall of the temple of Tirhakah, was built by a Roman emperor, because some columns and a dwarf wall, forming part of that structure, bear the figure and name of Cæsar, Titus, Ælius, Adrianus, Antoninus, Eusebes; nor is it matter of conjecture that the gateway, to which

XXII.—THE TEMPLE OF MEDINET-HABOU—THEBES.

it forms the right wing, was built by Ptolemy Lathyrus, because it likewise bears the figure and name of that king, and also of Dionysus or Auletes. Again, it is no matter of conjecture, although we have not precisely the same kind of evidence, that those brick ruins in the centre of our picture are the remains of the houses of the Christian inhabitants of this part of Thebes, from the first centuries of our era down to the Mohammedan conquest; because history tells us so, and because fragments of Christian books written on papyrus have been dug out of those ruins. Thus we have within the limits of this view, from the foreground to the statues in the plain, not a thousand yards distant, unequivocal historical landmarks ranging in time from the Mohammedan conquest back to the reign of Amunothph III.; that is to say, from the year 640 of our era to 1250 years before it.

J. B.

NOTE.—Tirhakah, the king whose name is upon the small temple with clustered columns, was the third of the Ethiopian kings who reigned over Egypt. The first was Sabacothph, who conquered Egypt in about B.C. 737. The second was Sevech or So, with whom Hoshea, King of Israel, formed alliance when threatened with an invasion by his powerful neighbour Shalmanezer King of Assyria. (See 2 Kings, xvii. 4.) The third Ethiopian was this king, Tirhakah, who came to the throne about B.C. 715. He formed an alliance with Hezekiah, King of Judah (see 2 Kings, xix. 9), and it would seem from Herodotus that it was against the forces of Tirhakah that the Assyrian army was encamped when it was miraculously destroyed in the night. The Bible does not say in what place this destruction took place: Herodotus says that it was near to Pelusium, the frontier town of Egypt.

Tirhakah, the Ethiopian, reigned in Egypt, while Hezekiah reigned in Judea, Sennacherib in Assyria, and Mardoch Empadus in Babylon; and with this last begins the series of recorded Babylonian eclipses, on which the historian now builds his chronology, while he acknowledges his debt to the Alexandrian astronomers who have preserved them for us, and to modern

XXII.—THE TEMPLE OF MEDINET-HABOU—THEBES.

science which has calculated them. The Egyptians kept no record of eclipses or of occultations of the stars.

Fig. 22.

Fig. 23.

Fig. 22 contains two forms of the hieroglyphical name of Ptolemy Soter II., often called Lathyrus; and fig. 23 is the hieroglyphical name of Ptolemy Neus Dionysus, often called Auletes.

S. S.

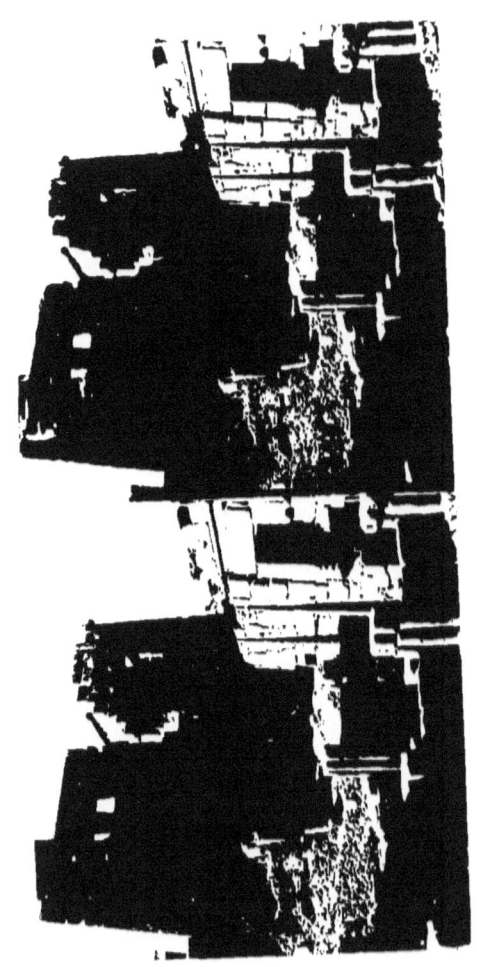

PLATE XXIII.

The Temple of Medinet-Habou—Near View.

This is a view of what is called the temple palace of Medinet-Habou. The square openings on that high building are the windows of small chambers, the walls of which are decorated with subjects of domestic import; to understand the form of this building, and its position with respect to the other buildings of Medinet-Habou, we must refer you to the plan (see fig. 24). You will perceive that a line, drawn through its centre, would likewise pass through the centre of the courts of the temple behind it. In this view, which is looking southward, we see the right wing of the entrance considerably dilapidated, and converted, by the early Christian inhabitants of Thebes, into a dwelling-house of many chambers, the beams of which were inserted into those rows of holes made in the masonry of the ancient structure. A little piece of the front of this building is seen to the left, and through that opening in the wall can be discerned the back of the court and the window of the chamber over the gate, the roof of which has been decorated with a row of shields. The cill of the opening in the side wall is supported by a row of Asiatic prisoners, over whom, as if trampling on his enemies, was, most likely, placed a movable statue of the warrior king who built this palace and temple, and who has decorated its walls with so many incised pictures, representing his conquest over various nations and peoples, more particu-

Fig. 24.

XXIII.—THE TEMPLE OF MEDINET-HABOU—NEAR VIEW.

larly to the north of Egypt. Fragments of statues made of wood, combined with other materials, have been found, such as might be supposed to have been placed out at this opening, and the opposite one, on state occasions, for the admiration of the Egyptian public. It will be observed, that over the two doors which gave access to the chambers at the back of the court there is a semicircle, showing that the ceilings of those passage chambers were of the arch form. Nearer the spectator are the ruins of houses, of the time of St. Anthony and St. Paul, the first Christian hermits who were natives of the Thebaid; and immediately in the foreground are the lower parts of the shafts of the columns of the temple of Tirhakah, with the connecting dwarf-wall. These columns are of an ancient form, of which we shall see more entire specimens. To the right is the gate leading to the court of a temple begun by Thothmes I., and carried on by his successors, Thothmes II. and III. On this gate the name of Tirhakah has been imperfectly effaced by Nectanebo, whose name appears in its place. Ptolemy Lathyrus has also appropriated a part of the walls of this court; and even Tirhakah himself, as it would appear, built up against this ancient gateway belonging to the first Thothmes. The size and form of this temple may be seen in the plan. It consists of a sanctuary enclosed on three sides by square pillars, joined by a dwarf wall; and on the fourth side are six small dark chambers. This part was begun by the first and second Thothmes, and completed in all its architectural details by the third, except the inscription on the outside of the architrave, which was added by Rameses III. Other names occur as the repairers of this ancient fane, among whom are those of Psammetichus II. and Achoris.

J. B.

Fig. 25.

NOTE.—Fig. 25 is the name of Nectanebo, above spoken of; he reigned about B.C. 380, and for eighteen years maintained the independence of Egypt against the invasion of the Persians.

S. S.

PLATE XXIV.

Osiride Columns of the Temple of Medinet-Habou.

WALKING from the place of the last view over the brick ruins that fill up the space between the palace of Rameses III. and the entrance to the first court of the temple, whose lintel and gate-posts are massive blocks of granite, and having entered the court, this view will present itself.

The roof of the portico on the right-hand side of the court is supported by seven colossal statues of Pharaoh Rameses III. in his military costume, bearing the crook and flail of Osiris, and wearing the kingly mitre of the same divinity. The backs of these statues are placed against massive piers which support the broad architrave stones and the diminished cornice: a marked feature in the architecture of this period. On the right side of the king is a statue of his son, and on the left that of his daughter, which will be better seen in the next photograph. On the opposite side of this court is a similar portico supported by seven columns, of the ancient order representing the fully expanded papyrus, of which we shall have occasion to speak when we have before us perfect specimens of the order. The right and left hand porticoes of this court are built up against the sloping sides of the towers of the first and second gateways, to which they are connected by a pilaster crowned with the curvetto and torus cornice. On the roof of both porticoes are the remains of the crude brick houses of the Christian inhabitants, probably belonging to persons connected with the cathedral church, which occupied the whole of the interior of the second court. Both the names of the Pharaoh can be distinctly made out on the side of each pillar. This may be the Egyptian conqueror of whom Herodotus says it was related of him that he tied captives to the wheels of his chariot, and that he was accompanied in battle by a lion. These two circumstances are distinctly recorded in the sculptures on the walls of the court, which was afterwards converted into a

XXIV.—OSIRIDE COLUMNS OF THE TEMPLE OF MEDINET-HABOU.

Christian place of worship. The heathen sculpture has been preserved, by having been covered with a coating of clay and lime, on which were painted Christian emblems.

J. B.

Note.—On the side of the pillar against which the statue leans, we see the name of Rameses III., the builder of this temple. Three kings of less note had reigned after the death of Rameses II., who have left us no great buildings; but Rameses III. would seem to have been a sovereign little less important than Rameses II. The painted sculptures on the walls proclaim his victories over neighbouring and also distant nations, and his triumphal and religious processions at home. He lived about the year B.C. 1050; but he was the last great king of Thebes. After him several others of the name followed as sovereigns of that city, and perhaps of the Thebaid; but it is doubtful whether any of them were kings of all Egypt. They built nothing; we find their names indeed on the older Theban buildings, but one only has left his name beyond the Thebaid, and so we may suppose that except in his case their power reached no farther.

Within a century from this time, we find Thebes ruled over by a king of Lower Egypt, Shishank of Bubastis, who conquered Rehoboam, and is mentioned in 1 Kings xi. 40; xiv. 25.

S. S.

PLATE XXV.

Near View of Osiride Columns of the Temple of Medinet-Habou.

A TOLERABLE notion of the colossal dimensions of this statue can be obtained from the figure of the Arab boatman standing on the rubbish and leaning against the pier. On the wall behind the pier may be seen the elaborate and highly historical incised and painted decoration belonging to this portico of the first court of the temple. Besides that feature in the architecture of this period already noticed, viz. the great width of the architrave stone and the smallness of the cornice, is that of the deeply incised hieroglyphics and sculpture. This particular feature is admirably exhibited in the photograph, in the elaborate inscription on the sloping surface of the tower of the pylon, and in those two lines of colossal hieroglyphics near the base of the wall. The lower part of this statue has only lately been brought to light—probably not seen since the temple was converted into a Christian place of worship; at which time, it is probable, the hands and face of the statue were battered. The excavation discloses another kind of defacement which must have been done before the ground had attained its present level, and that is those furrows in the left foot. The perpetrators of this defacement seem to have had some other purpose in view than the mere wanton defacement of the statue. We shall be better able to judge of this matter when we have seen other examples of the like defacement.

J. B.

NOTE.—This colossal statue has had its beard violently and purposely broken off, as is the case with almost all the Egyptian statues. The nature of the mutilation is so remarkable, that we are able to guess with tolerable certainty who were the authors of it. The Persians, who conquered Egypt under Cambyses in B.C. 533, held their beards in great reverence, and thought they could show no greater insult to the statues of Egypt than by aiming their blow at the chin. By destroying the beard, they robbed the statue of its mark of manhood.

S. S.

The foot of King Amunothph III. trampling on his enemies, alternately Arabs and Ethiopians.

THE TEMPLE OF THE SET HEART, TEOTE

XXV

PLATE XXVI.

New Excavations of Medinet-Habou.

To understand this view we must again refer to the plan (see Plate 23). It will be seen that the view is taken from the back part of the temple, the photographist standing on the rubbish thrown out of the adjacent chambers. By reference to the plans of all the more ancient temples, a similarity of design will be recognized; and it will be observed that a series of small chambers are placed behind the larger one, commonly called the hall of columns, and that these are multiplied with a curious complication at the sides as well as behind the hall. It will likewise be observed that a larger space is given to these mysterious chambers in the temple of Medinet-Habou than to any of the other of the more ancient temples, and that the great hall contains only ten rows of columns, the two centre being, as usual, of the taller order, by which a clerestory was obtained, giving abundance of light. The smaller chambers were probably lighted by an aperture in the ceiling, as there are no openings in the side walls for this purpose.

From this view some idea of the great perfection and elegance of the decoration of an Egyptian temple may be formed. Not a single foot of unmeaning wall—every part has its appropriate, intelligible decoration, expressed in the universal language of art and the vernacular of Egypt, by means of those highly decorative and pictorial characters, with which the learned of Europe are every day becoming better acquainted. The walls of the larger and the surrounding smaller chambers speak to us of the religious actions and mysteries of the ancient Egyptians; but the walls of the court, to which that door gives entrance, speak of conquests and public ceremonies, and religious processions, which were conducted through those very courts to that door, the people being congregated in the courts under the portico, but not admitted beyond the dwarf wall which bounds that side of this second court

XXVI.—NEW EXCAVATIONS IN THE COURTS OF MEDINET-HABOU.

to which that door leads. In one of these processions, the king is seated on a throne carried on the shoulders of men and surrounded by the officers of his court, among whom are the bearers of two semicircular fans, apparently made of feathers, and resembling in form the flabelli, carried in the processions with the Roman pontiff; to whom also, as in these sculptures, they offer incense.

The extent of this second court is marked by the two first towers, to which a small door gives access from the roof of the portico into the left tower. The next high building is the left tower of the first propylon, of which two square openings near the gate are for sustaining flag-poles that were erected on certain festive occasions. To the right are the crude brick walls of the houses of the Christian village, which extended over the whole of this recently excavated part of the ancient structure.

J. B.

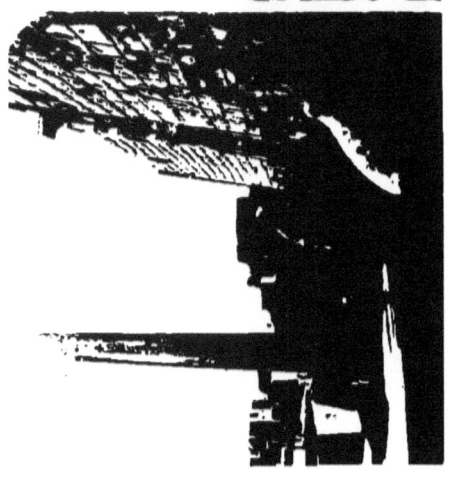

PLATE XXVII.

The Temple of Luxor—Thebes—The Obelisk.

THIS view is the first that presents itself on arriving from the opposite side of the river, and the most conspicuous object in it is the companion obelisk to that in the Place de la Concorde, in Paris. This extraordinary work of science and art, like that in Paris, is of the time of the predecessor of that Pharaoh whose temple we have just examined at Medinet-Habou. The entire height of the single block of granite of which this obelisk is made is about eighty feet. Great as the weight of this single block of stone must be, it is not more than two-thirds of the large obelisk of Karnak, nor more than a quarter of the weight of the colossal statue of the Memnonium, the work of the same Pharaoh.

Pliny gives an account of how these enormous blocks of granite were brought from the quarries of Syene, and there is an Egyptian picture representing the moving of a colossal statue; but as yet we have no account of how they were erected on their pedestals, except so far as now, for the first time, explained by the woodcut in the margin, (fig. 26). The obelisks of Luxor, as may be fairly conjectured by the groove in the pedestal being on that side of it nearest the river, were brought by water and landed on a raised platform, by which means one angle of its base was brought exactly over the groove. The next process was to raise the block, and this could now be done without any danger of slipping, or, in other words, with a certainty of its turning in the groove, as it were in

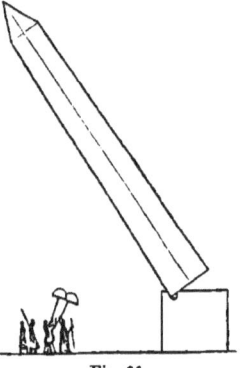

Fig. 26.

XXVII.—THE TEMPLE OF LUXOR—THEBES—THE OBELISK.

a hinge, till it had attained so nearly a perpendicular as to require a support below the base. This was probably given to it by confining a quantity of sand on the top of the pedestal, which sand was gradually allowed to run off till the obelisk attained the perpendicular position.

Precisely by the same process, 200 years before, were the statues in the plain set up, as the groove in the pedestals testifies : the only questionable part being the means employed in raising and lowering.

The pyramidion on the top of this obelisk and its companion being left rough and unadorned with sculpture, it is conjectured it was covered with a bronze cap. Then follows a square compartment, in which the king is represented making offerings to Amun-ra; and then three vertical columns of admirable hieroglyphics, the centre column being the best in form and execution, on all the four sides of this and its companion in Paris.

It will be observed, by a glance at the plan, that besides the two obelisks, there are four colossal statues sitting in front of the entrance to this temple ; and nearly behind each are the groove and square opening, two in each tower, for sustaining the flag-staffs already alluded to, and which we shall have a better opportunity of explaining in another view (see fig. 27).

The whole exterior surface of the more distant tower of this gateway, from the two square openings down to the top of the grooves, is occupied with the incised picture of the same battle scene of the fortified city surrounded by water, already described as repeated twice on the walls of the Memnonium ; and the whole of the surface of the nearest tower, within the same limits, is occupied by the encampment scene. Those little notches, that look in this oblique view like the teeth of a saw, are formed by the rounded heads of the shields of the Egyptian soldiers placed together forming the boundary of the camp. Higher and nearer the gate is the colossal incised figure of the king sitting at the door of his tent, receiving the congratulations of his subjects who have come out to meet him on his return from the conquest of this important fenced city of an Asiatic people, of light complexion, to the north of Egypt.

Behind

XXVII.—THE TEMPLE OF LUXOR—THEBES—THE OBELISK.

Fig. 27.

XXVII.—THE TEMPLE OF LUXOR—THEBES—THE OBELISK.

Behind the king, and within the encampment, are the prisoners and spoil of the conquered city, and the very same incidents repeated as in the picture on the inner surface of the left tower of the propylon of the Memnonium. Below the pictures of both towers is a long inscription, in many lines of perpendicular hieroglyphics; no doubt a full account of the whole campaign against these powerful enemies of Egypt: judging from the pains taken to record this conquest three times on the walls of the temples of Thebes alone, it must have been the most important event in the reign of Rameses II. We shall have occasion to return to this subject, as this record is again repeated on the walls of the great chamber of the larger excavated temple of Abusimbel.

The buildings behind the obelisk, with inclined walls, are the houses of the present inhabitants of this district of Thebes. On the top of these are contrivances for the accommodation and preservation of pigeons; consisting of four small towers, perforated with cells for each pair, and furnished with the slender branches of trees for the more commodious alighting.

J. B.

PLATE XXVIII.

The Temple of Luxor—Thebes. Head of Colossal Statue near the Entrance.

In this view, looking towards the west, we have a good opportunity of judging of the colossal dimensions of the statue by the figure sitting on its shoulder.

The obelisk now in Paris stood in the same relation to this statue as that which we saw in the last view does to the companion statue on the left-hand of the entrance (see Plan, fig. 28). This colossus was excavated to its base at the time of the removal of the obelisk by the French engineer M. Lebas, and it was found to be a sitting figure about twenty-five feet high, carved out of a single block of black granite. It represents Rameses II., as the hieroglyphics on the stem at the back, which takes the form of an obelisk, inform us.

The right door-jamb, which we see in this view, has on the front Rameses II. making an offering to Amun-ra and Mout. In the compartment above this sculpture there remains only the figure of Rameses, and the compartment below is too much defaced to make out; but in the compartment on the surface at right angles to the last, we have a representation of the king being received by one of the divinities of the temple, who, as it were, welcomes him at the threshold of the sacred edifice. The lower compartment on this surface

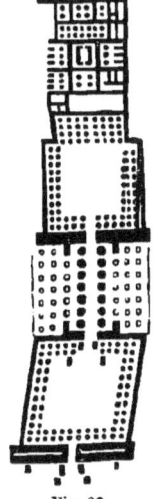

Fig. 28.

is likewise too defaced to describe; but we may remark that the sculptures on this surface are in true basso-rilievo, whereas those on the front surface are in

XXVIII.—THE TEMPLE OF LUXOR—THEBES.

that kind of rilievo peculiar to Egypt, which of all kinds of sculpture is that which is best adapted for enduring; because the contour or outline of the figure being the deepest part of the work is the last to be destroyed in the ordinary wear and tear of ages. It is not, however, as we see, proof against the iconoclastic fury of the Christians of the first centuries, who converted this building into a church; or it may be the Mahommedan invaders, who have battered out the features of all three of the otherwise best preserved figures on the front of the door-jamb. Just above the cap of the colossus, on the front of the gate-tower, can be discerned a row of figures, which are those of the principal inhabitants of Thebes, headed by one of the officers of the court going up to congratulate his majesty on his safe return to the capital. The figure of the king is not so distinctly seen; he is seated on a chair of state, and attired in a robe of ceremony, extending his right hand in sign of approval towards the officer who approaches the throne in respectful attitude. No small force or little labour was employed to batter out the features and split the top of the upper crown of the granite colossus. This larger destruction was probably the work of the Babylonish invaders under Nebuchadnezzar, or the soldiers of Cambyses, to whom in the time of Strabo the inhabitants of Thebes attributed all such masterpieces of violence and wanton destruction.

J. B.

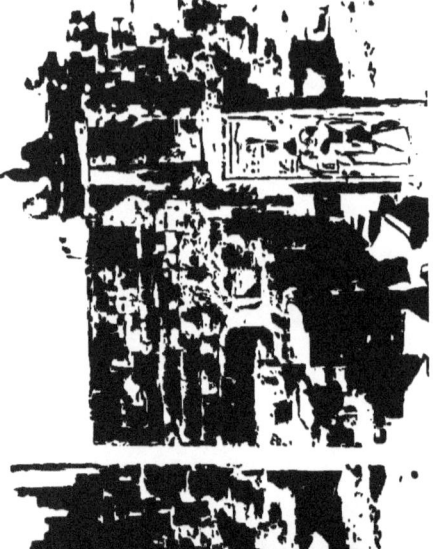

THE TEMPLE OF KARNAK - PILLARS

PLATE XXIX.

The Temple of Karnak, Thebes — Central Avenue.

This view down the centre avenue of the great temple of Alkarnak is taken from the roof of the granite sanctuary, and looking directly west. So vast and intricate is this wonderful ruin, that we shall have to make frequent reference to the plan, to profit adequately by these admirable photographs (see Plan, fig. 29). The nearest object in this view is a square granite block, bearing a figure of the goddess Mout, who receives in a most affectionate manner Pharaoh Thothmes II. at the threshold of the granite sanctuary. Another similar granite block stands at the other side of the entrance to the sanctuary. This subject, namely, a representation of the Pharaoh being received by the divinities of the temple, occupies the front and back surfaces of both the long square blocks of granite; while the other two surfaces bear the figures of the papyrus of Upper and Lower Egypt; that belonging to Lower Egypt being sculptured on the block to the north: that belonging to Upper Egypt being sculptured on the block to the south.

The next conspicuous stones are those of the windows of the clerestory, standing on the cornice of the smaller columns of the Great Hall. They stand

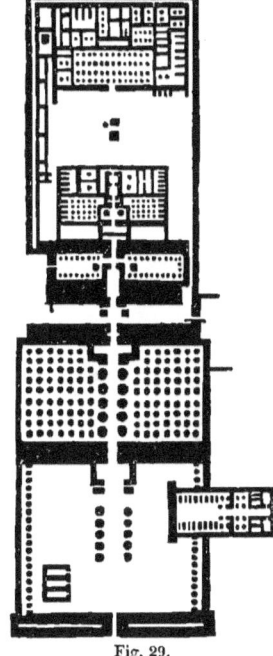

Fig. 29.

XXIX.—THE TEMPLE OF KARNAK, THEBES—CENTRAL AVENUE.

edgewise, and do not show us the opening of the window. Then we have the point of an obelisk, called the smaller obelisk of Karnak, seen over the architrave stones of the gate. Lastly, the tower of the great entrance of the temple from the west, or from the hill. One of the upper square perforations is to be seen for the attachment of the flag-poles already spoken of in the temple of Medinet-Habou. In this great propylon of the principal temple of Thebes, there appears to have been provision for the erection of four of these flag-poles against each tower, and each secured by two square perforations. This part of the edifice, however, was never finished.

J. B.

PLATE XXX.

Columns and Part of the Obelisk of Thothmosis ii. —Karnak, Thebes.

CONTINUING our walk in a westerly direction, down the centre avenue, past the sandstone gateway, so conspicuous in the two former views, we arrive at the smaller obelisk. The eastern and southern surfaces of the obelisk are presented to us, and it will be easy to perceive, from the well-defined and elegant forms of the hieroglyphics of the centre column, that it is of a different period to those on each side of it; and we shall be confirmed in that conjecture by an examination of the characters contained in the ovals. The conspicuous oval in the centre line of the east face contains the hieroglyphics of the name of Thothmosis I. (see fig. 30), who lived 1390 years before our era, or fifty or sixty years before Moses; while the ovals in the side lines contain the hieroglyphics of the name of Rameses IV. and V. It will also be easy to perceive that the surface of the granite at the place where the word Amun occurs, in the centre line, has been lowered. This is another example bearing upon that particular change in the religious sentiments of the Egyptians to which we have already alluded; while in the

Fig. 30.

side lines we have an example of obliterations in the hieroglyphics contained in the ovals, indicating a change in the political opinions of the people, or a desire on the part of the monarch Rameses V. to appropriate to himself the titles and honours claimed by his predecessor, Rameses IV. The roof of stones and other fragments that encumbered the centre avenue have lately been cleared away, and the larger columns, which supported the higher part of the roof, uncovered to their bases. The two nearest of these columns were

XXX.—COLUMNS AND PART OF THE OBELISK OF THOTHMOSIS II.

attached, as the plan informs us, to the massive construction of the gate, which was thereby connected with what there is reason to believe at one time formed an exterior gate, with towers, in front of the sanctuary, for the adornment of which this obelisk and its fallen companion were erected by Thothmosis, and that the immense hall of columns was an addition made by Oimenepthah I. or Rameses II. The columns of this centre avenue are 66 feet high, and of that beautiful order representing the fully-expanded papyrus.

The circumference of the largest part of the capital is exactly the length of the column from the top of the base to the bottom of the abacus. From the neck of the capital the shaft gradually widens till about three feet from the base (where it measures 12 feet); it then rapidly decreases to nearly the same width as it is at the neck, namely, 9 feet 6 inches; imitating the contraction in the stem of the papyrus, which it further resembles by its being clothed with tight-fitting leaves, as we shall see in the next photograph. To the right, between the columns of the centre avenue and the obelisk, are the shorter columns, the first row of which support the piers of the windows of the clerestory. These columns are 40 feet high; they represent the bud of the papyrus, and carry out the resemblance to the natural plant at that stage of its growth, in the same architectonic mode as the larger columns. Of these columns there are 112 which support the lower roof, and 22 which support the roof of the clerestory, making in all 134. We shall see, as we advance farther into this chamber, that all the columns are covered with painted sculpture and hieroglyphics as well as its walls, by which means one-third more surface than the walls themselves furnished was acquired for significant decoration, conveying an amount of historical and religious knowledge that the temples of no other people convey. Thus, too, ample compensation was made for the loss of space taken up by the great number and massiveness of the columns.

On the second column of the right hand may be seen a full-length of Amun-ra, to whom Rameses II. presents an offering. On the third column the same Rameses makes an offering to the divinity Khem, by whom, not improbably, the Egyptians meant to designate the great antediluvian

XXX.—COLUMNS AND PART OF THE OBELISK OF THOTHMOSIS II.

father of their race, Ham. On the fourth column Amun again appears, and on the fifth Khem; so that, in walking down this avenue towards the west, you were met by Rameses offering alternately to those two great divinities, and in walking up the avenue in an easterly direction you were met by the divinities of the temple.

To the left of the avenue is a sloping piece of masonry, which is part of the tower that flanks the entrance into the hall on the left.

J. B.

NOTE.—In the second oval of king Thothmosis I. (see fig 30), the ibis on a perch, is the word Thoth, the threefold character is M, and the horizontal character is S, thus forming his name. Of the three smaller characters crowded in, that formed of two semicircles, perhaps an anvil, is the word Mes; the looped character, a musical instrument, is H, or Ho; and the sun is Ra, or with the article, Phra; and the three form the word Meshophra. This agrees very satisfactorily with his name in Manetho's list, where he is called Misaphris, and where his successor, who has two names nearly the same also in the second oval, is called Misphragmuthosis, evidently meant for Mishophra-thothmosis.

Rameses IV. and V. here mentioned, are two kings whose names are not known out of Thebes, and in Thebes are no monuments of their own raising. When they were there reigning, the power of Upper Egypt was lessened, and that of Lower Egypt was rising; and these two were probably kings only of the Thebaid.

S. S.

PLATE XXXI.

Columns of the Temple of Karnak — Thebes.

THIS view is taken from between the first columns at the east end of the hall, which, as before stated, were attached by solid masonry to the gate piers. We see between these columns obliquely across the central avenue, having before us a succession of the smaller columns, which support the lower roof. The column next to the two immediately in the foreground, is the same as the second of the right-hand row in the last view; but being so much closer, the details of the sculpture are more defined, and we see more distinctly the supplicating position of the king, as contrasted with the very upright figure of the god, to whom he offers something in two vases similar in form to the one on the small altar before him. Above this representation, to the neck of the capital, the shaft is decorated with the names of the king. Below the representation is a band of large hieroglyphics, in which the name and titles of Rameses II. are conspicuous, while a little removed from it is a band of small, deeply cut hieroglyphics, in which the name and titles of the Pharaoh of Medinet-Habou occur, and no doubt added in his reign. Below this a band of ornaments, which addresses itself to the eye alone, representing little squares of different colours, contained in a black frame-work; below that again, the beginning of one of those close-fitting leaves, which embrace the lower part of the column, as they do the natural plant. At the point where the brick restoration commences, the shaft begins to contract, and here very happily is placed the figure of a living descendant of Mizraim, affording us opportunity of estimating the colossal dimensions of the column and of the figures engraved on the shaft of it. The architrave stone of the smaller order is decorated with an inscription in two lines, and in the curvetto should be seen the king's oval, alternating with a triple ornament—from which, not improbably, the triglyph of the Greek temple was devised.

J. B.

PLATE XXXII.

Hall of the Temple of Karnak — Thebes.

THIS is a view taken from the northern end of the transverse avenue of columns looking southwards. The mind of the thinking observer is afflicted with a sentiment of melancholy in wandering among these stupendous ruins, and particularly at this point of view, when so much magnificence and devastation are brought together in one picture.

To understand the position from which this extraordinary scene is taken, we must refer you to the plan. Placing oneself in imagination in the middle of the transverse avenue, and in the fifth from the centre, this view will present itself. It is remarkable for exhibiting the structure of a window in what is called the clerestory in Gothic buildings, which, as we shall perceive, is made of an upper and lower slab of sandstone, perforated with thirteen long furrows, leaving twelve bars of somewhat greater width than the openings. In the lower slab several more of these bars have been knocked out than in the upper one, with a view of completing more promptly the destruction of this part of the temple—such has been the malignity of the efforts of the invader to root out all memory of this extraordinary people. Three avenues beyond that of the clerestory is a column leaning against its opposite neighbour, not owing so much to human violence as to a very curious chemical action going on at the base of the walls and columns of all the sandstone temples of Thebes, produced by the nitrous earth which has accumulated about their foundations. In the columns of the foreground this chemical action has been arrested by the brick restoration, and a similar catastrophe to that on the other side, deferred at least for some years; for which we are indebted to the forethought and prudence of M. Mariette, who has likewise rendered many other important services to the students in Egyptian history.

XXXII.—HALL OF THE TEMPLE OF KARNAK—THEBES.

There seems to have been an insatiable desire in the Hamitic race to hand down to posterity the memory of their existence. To nothing but that characteristic feature of the Egyptian mind can be attributed that untiring diligence with which a sovereign repeated his name on every column of a structure of these vast proportions. To gratify this propensity, none of the smaller columns on this side the central avenue have escaped an alteration in the original decoration, as may be seen in this photograph.

Fig. 31.

Over the five horizontal bands at the neck of the capital has been cut a royal legend, containing the names of Pharaoh Rameses IV., and likewise over the pendent fascia below the horizontal bands, as may be seen by those perpendicular furrows dividing the ovals (see fig. 31). Again, a legend containing the same name encircles the column below the pendants. Then follows the original sculptured representation of the founder, making offerings to the gods; but below that is a band of large hieroglyphics, containing the name of Rameses II., who had already appropriated all the plain spaces on the larger columns, as we shall see in some of the succeeding photographs. In the British Museum there is a granite column, representing a cluster of papyrus-buds of the time of Pharaoh Amunothph III., which 150 years after was disfigured all over with the name of a son of Rameses II.

This specimen, in our national collection, is also a monument of that change in the religious opinions of the Egyptians already alluded to, in that the second oval containing the name of that Pharaoh has been obliterated, because compounded of the word Amun, which was afterwards restored to it, when that divinity came again into favour. The precise time of this return to favour is not known, but there is reason to believe, as the names of Amun Mai Rameses have never suffered obliteration, it may have been during his reign or a little previous to it.

The floor of the hall has been disencumbered of the fragments of architrave and roof stones nearly to the top of the bases of the columns; and we have by means of the figure of the living descendant of Mizraim, standing in the central avenue, a tolerable notion of the stupendous

XXXII.—HALL OF THE TEMPLE OF KARNAK—THEBES.

architecture of this hall, to which there is no ancient or modern structure that can be compared, either for the consistent, harmonious, instructive decoration, or the vastness of its dimensions.

J. B.

Note.—Rameses IV., who has added his name to this building of his great ancestor, as has been before remarked, is a king almost unknown to us. We can find no temples, or even parts of temples, built during his reign. We do not even find his name out of Thebes. We are led to conjecture that the power and wealth of his family were much lessened when he came to the throne. We afterwards find the name of Rameses VII. at Memphis; and it would seem as if the kings between Rameses III. and Rameses VII. were not kings of all Egypt, but of Thebes only.

S. S.

PLATE XXXIII.

Temple of Karnak — View from the Top of Hall.

THIS view is taken from the roof of the lower part of the Hall, looking eastward. Enormous blocks, covered with speaking decoration, hurled down chiefly by human violence, cucumber, the foreground. Farther in are two columns, which support the piers—between which we have a back view of the same window tracery we saw in the last picture. Over the next opening are the holes for the beams of the roof of a chamber, which probably some hermit like Stylites occupied till the Mohammedan invasion or the corroding nitre warned him to quit. Through this opening, and the one to the left, are seen the capitals of the columns of the centre avenue; farther on, the solitary and dangerous pier of a fifth window: then the smaller and larger obelisk; beyond this the top of the gate, so conspicuous in two former views; and lastly the date groves, and mountains of the eastern desert, in the direction of Elcosseyr, the port of Thebes on the coast of the Red Sea.

The papyrus-bud columns on this side the centre avenue have not been disfigured with the names of those later members of the family of the great Rameses, like those we saw in the last photograph; but the light being so directly opposite, neither the horizontal bands of the upper part of the shaft nor the vertical lines of the fascia are clearly discernible. They are, however, precisely as shown in the wood-cut of photograph 32.

The smaller of the two obelisks in this view is that which we saw in Plate 29, and of which we saw the side in Plate 30. It is second in size to that in the Piazza S. Giovanni Laterano in Rome, that being 102 feet, and this being 93 feet. It is the longest single block of granite in the whole world; the companion obelisk lies broken into numerous fragments, as well as the companion of that smaller obelisk whose apex is just seen above the architrave stones of the gate. The hierogly-

XXXIII.—TEMPLE OF KARNAK—VIEW FROM THE TOP OF HALL.

phical inscriptions on both these obelisks have been published in Burton's *Excerpta Hieroglyphica*, by Rosellini, and by Lepsius; and there is a model of the larger one done to scale in the mummy room of the British Museum. The apex of the larger obelisk is adorned with hieroglyphics, and a representation of the person who erected it being crowned by the great divinity of Thebes, Amun-ra. The sides are sculptured in compartments, representing figures of a king making offerings to the same divinity; while down the centre is a single line of admirably sculptured hieroglyphics. Not only is this obelisk one of the most remarkable works of art in the world, on account of the beauty of the forms sculptured on it, and one of the most remarkable works of science, not having been raised on its base in the manner of those of Luxor, but by some other means of which we have no conception; but it is also remarkable in an historical point of view, for since it was erected in the place it still occupies, there was a time when certain divinities of Egypt fell into disrepute, and in consequence of this change in the religious opinions, their names and figures were artistically erased and subsequently restored, wherever they occurred on this obelisk, and on every other monument throughout the country. To effect this, scaffoldings must have been erected about all the obelisks, and against the walls of all the temples which were standing at the time of the first and again at the time of the second change. The circumstances which induced these changes in the religious opinions of the ancient Egyptians are entirely unknown, as also the precise time and interval between the erasure and reinsertion of certain names; yet they must have been considered of importance, otherwise so much pains and expense would not have been incurred to make these documents, public as they were, tally so precisely with them; and therefore it would be very desirable that future travellers should examine the monuments with a view to detect them wherever they occur, by which means the circumstances connected with each particular erasure and insertion might be reasonably conjectured. Hitherto, owing to the consummate artistic skill with which both erasures and insertions have been effected, on hard or soft stones alike, they have escaped observation.

J. B.

XXXIII.—TEMPLE OF KARNAK.—VIEW FROM THE TOP OF HALL.

NOTE.—The obelisk described by Mr. Bonomi is the tallest in Egypt, and at the same time in all probability the oldest, because those which bear the name of Osirtesen I. were most likely made by his namesake, Nectanebo. The inscriptions upon it are published in Burton's *Excerpta Hieroglyphica*. On the middle of the three lines of writing which run down its face, it bears the names of Thothmosis I. and of Queen Mikera Amun-Nitocris, wife of Thothmosis II. On the two side lines of writing it bears the names of Thothmosis III. and of the same queen. This very important lady was thus the colleague of two kings; and her inscriptions and history are not a little curious.

1st. Eratosthenes translates her name Nitocris, as *Minerva the victorious*, which is part of her second oval (see fig. 32) spelt N T, Neith; T R, or ChR, *victorious*. The Egyptian T has occasionally, as in this name, the force of a guttural, and hence we find a confusion between it and the Ch or G. Eratosthenes further says that she governed Egypt for her husband, which quite agrees with what we learn from the inscriptions, from which she would seem to have been the governor of the kingdom during the greater part of two reigns.

Fig. 32.

2nd. Strange to say, this lady, whose titles are always feminine, as "mistress of the world, daughter of the sun," is here always sculptured in man's clothes (see fig. 33), a circumstance which we find explained by learning, that while wife of Thothmosis II. (see fig. 34), king of Thebes, she was also a sovereign in her own right.

3rd. Manetho tells us that Queen Nitocris was the last of the line of independent sovereigns of Memphis, and the builder of the third pyramid. Hence we learn from this obelisk, that it was her marriage with Thothmosis II. that united Upper and Lower Egypt under one sceptre. This lady was queen consort of Upper Egypt and queen regnant of Lower Egypt.

Fig. 34.

Fig. 33.

XXXIII.—TEMPLE OF KARNAK.—VIEW FROM THE TOP OF HALL.

4th. We moreover learn from numerous other inscriptions, that this union of the two kingdoms was not brought about without some jealousy. For in most cases we find that when the name of Nitocris is met with on a tablet, joined to that of either of her colleagues, Thothmosis II. or Thothmosis III., one or other of the two names has been purposely cut out. Those who were attached to the Theban king destroyed the name of Nitocris, and those who were attached to the Memphite queen destroyed the name of Thothmosis.

5th. Herodotus tells us, in apparent contradiction to Manetho, that the third pyramid was built by King Mycerinus. And when the third and fourth pyramids were lately opened, the name of King Mekora (see fig. 35) was found in both of them, with no mention of Queen Nitocris. But this contradiction may possibly be explained. Let us suppose that as Thothmosis and Nitocris were both sovereigns in their own right, one of Thebes and the other of Memphis, the two pyramids, the third and the fourth, may have been made one for each. The name of Mekora, found in each, though spelt with different characters, is nearly the same in sound as the first name of Queen Nitocris (see fig. 32), and hence it may have been the name used at Memphis by Thothmosis.

6th, and lastly. Manetho's information is in part supported by Herodotus himself; for he tells us that some said that this third pyramid was built by a woman of the reign of King Amasis. His information confounds Nitocris, the queen of Thothmosis II., with Nitocris the mother-in-law of Amasis; for we find from the inscriptions that the queen of Amasis was the daughter of a Queen Neith-acoret, or Nitocris. Thus the two accounts which were given to Herodotus are reconciled by our finding that Mikera, the colleague of Thothmosis, whom we suppose to be Mycerinus, and the mother-in-law of Amasis, were both named Nitocris.

We further add the hieroglyphical name of King Thothmosis III. (see fig. 36), which is on the side lines of this obelisk; and it will be seen that the guttural sound, which is always so puzzling to nations who do not use it, will reconcile his first name with that found in the third pyramid. The one is spelt Me-ho-ra and the other Me-ko-ra (see fig. 35). The beetle is Ho,

XXXIII.—TEMPLE OF KARNAK.—VIEW FROM THE TOP OF HALL.

and the three pairs of arms are Ko. At the same time the single pair of arms in the queen's name is Ka, making her first name Mi-ka-ra.

Fig. 35.

Fig. 36.

The first name of Thothmosis III., which we have been reading Me-ho-ra (see fig. 36), is also sometimes spelt Men-ho-ra; and as the article Ph is often added in pronunciation before Ra, *the sun*, it was then pronounced Menhophra. And it is from this name that we learn the date of this king, Thothmosis III., and thence the dates of all the great kings of Thebes. The Sothic period of 1460 years, or four times 365 years, was the time during which the civil New Year's Day travelled all round the natural year for want of an intercalary day and a leap-year. This period came to an end in the year A.D. 138, in the beginning of the reign of Antoninus Pius; and it began 1460 years earlier, in A.D. 1322. The time when it began was traditionally called the Era of Menhophra, and hence we learn this date of King Thothmosis III.

By the help of this date, we fix, with some little probability, the dates of the other early Egyptian kings: first, as Manetho tells us that Queen Nitocris was the twelfth sovereign of Memphis after Chofo, we learn, by allowing about twenty-seven and a half years to a reign, that the oldest pyramid was built between B.C. 1700 and B.C. 1600; this we have already explained, when describing the pyramids, at Plate III. Secondly; the Tablet of Abydos tells us that Rameses II. was seventh sovereign of Thebes after Thothmosis III., which would place Rameses II. between B.C. 1200 and B.C. 1100.

We find no record in Egypt that tells us which was the king who drove

XXXIII.—TEMPLE OF KARNAK.—VIEW FROM THE TOP OF HALL.

out the Israelites under Moses; and the Bible only tells us that he was called Pharaoh, *the king*, a title common to all. Hence we must determine it as well as we can by the circumstances told us in the Bible.

1st. When Joseph's brethren came down into Egypt, the Shepherds were an abomination in the eyes of the Egyptians (Gen. xlvi. 34). Hence the war which had driven out that hated people was already past, and not forgotten. It was, therefore, after the reign of Amosis of Thebes, who freed Egypt from those foreigners.

2nd. Four generations after, a king had arisen in Egypt who knew not Joseph (Exod. i. 8); who had never heard of the services which he had rendered to the former king of Lower Egypt, and which had earned so much favour for his family. This king, who ill-treated the Israelites and wished to have their male children killed at their birth, must have been of a new race altogether; and such a king we find in Thothmosis III. Lower Egypt, since the death of Nitocris, who had carried that kingdom to Thothmosis II., king of Thebes, was no longer governed by a native sovereign. The king of Thebes may well have been ignorant of what the kings of Lower Egypt owed to Joseph. This then fixes the reign in which Moses was born. It was under Thothmosis III. The brick of unburnt clay, represented at fig. 37, bears the stamp of his name, and is such a one as the Israelites were required to make (Exod. i. 14).

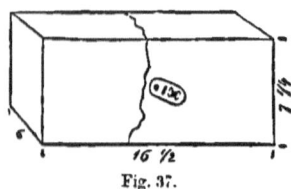

Fig. 37.

Before the departure of the Israelites from Egypt, we read that, "the King of Egypt died" (Exod. xi. 23); hence it was probably his son and successor, Amunothph II., whose chariots pursued Moses, and were overthrown in the Red Sea.

S. S.

PLATE XXXIV.

Temple of Karnak :—with Colonnade.

THIS is a view taken from the top of the lower roof of the hall, and looking northwards across the centre avenue. The two columns on the right hand are those nearest the western entrance to the hall; and the sloping wall on the left is that of the two towers of the gate. From this point we are made acquainted with the beautiful form of the capital, representing the expanded filaments of the papyrus plant—that important production of the Nile, which gave to Egypt, at so early a period, such incalculable advantages. At the base of the capital can be discovered those fibrous leaves that surround, in the same way, the root of the filaments in the natural plant. Many of these capitals retain a great deal of the colour by which the beauty of the form was enhanced; but the deep shadow of the projecting rim obscures the lines by which these forms and colours were bounded, and also a series of ovals containing the names of Rameses II. with which these capitals are adorned. Below the capital are the five bands, the second and fourth of which are painted blue; and under the fifth is a narrow cavity likewise painted blue, representing the heavens. Below this last are the ovals containing the hieroglyphics of the names of Rameses II., the sacred asp between each, which like the oval is surmounted by a red disk and feathers; while below the oval is that vase-like hieroglyphic, which is significant of the precious metals. (See fig. 38). Then follows an enriched border, and then another blue band significative of the heavens; under which, again, the ovals of Rameses II. surmounted with the disk and feathers of Truth, but without the intervening serpent. Then follows the sculpture representing Oimenepthah (see fig. 9) making offerings to the principal divinities of the temple; namely, Khem and Amun-ra. On the left is the sloping wall of the

TEMPLE OF KARNAK :—WITH COLONNADE.

towers of the western entrance to this hall of columns. Beyond, a series of the smaller columns which supported the lower roof; and, lastly, a piece of the north flank wall of enormous thickness, in which is an ample staircase to the roof. From the north face of this wall, at this point, was taken the

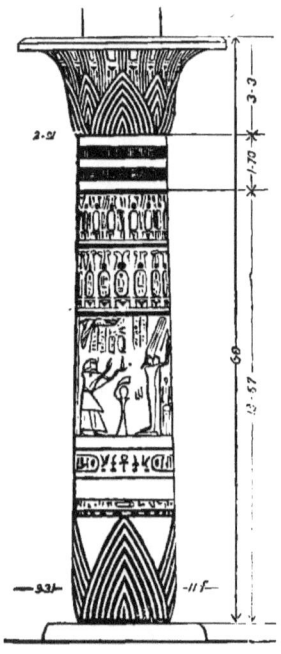

Fig. 38.

cast on the landing of the staircase of the British Museum, representing Oimenepthah I. subduing those persevering enemies of Egypt who are called Talmai in some of the inscriptions: a race of people of light complexion, blue eyes, and gigantic stature, and wearing two remarkable locks

XXXIV.—TEMPLE OF KARNAK:—WITH COLONNADE.

of hair. (See fig. 39.) The sculptures on the outside of this wall are in admirable preservation, owing to the northern surface being less subject to those vicissitudes of temperature which affect the southern wall. Both, however, are decorated with a series of sculptures of the greatest historical interest, representing chiefly incidents of battle with various peoples, in which the sovereign was personally engaged. There are three series of these large Egyptian riliovi, only a few of which have been drawn, and many not yet completely uncovered.

Fig. 39.

J. B.

NOTE.—The bands marked by the sculptor round these columns, immediately below the capital, are here out of place; they are a borrowed ornament taken from the column which imitates a cluster of papyrus stalks, in which the sculptured bands represent those which would be needed to hold a cluster of stalks together. In the case of this column, which is in imitation of a single stalk of papyrus, no bands are needed. By the same mode of reasoning we may judge that the capital of a Greek column is borrowed from this Egyptian column, which is a papyrus stalk, and naturally bears a papyrus flower at the top; but the Greek column is not the stem of a plant, and yet its capital is sometimes formed of leaves as if it were so. The Greek column also has a fillet or band round it, which is only in its true place on a column of clustered stalks.

The Arabs, against whom Oimenepthah I. is fighting, as described by Mr. Bonomi, do not seem always to have been enemies of Egypt. Other inscriptions count them among the four races of subjects; namely, Ethiopians, Thebans or Copts, Lower Egyptians, and Arabs.

S. S.

PLATE XXXV.

Temple of Karnak.—Columns with Capitals in Imitation of full-blown Papyrus.

Two of the same columns appear in this view that were described in the last; but here, in the more distant one, we have almost a geometrical delineation of the beautiful curve which the Egyptian architect has given to the profile of this capital, as well as further details of the ornament engraved on its surface; namely, the leaves at the base of the capital, and the ascending filaments terminating in flowers and buds. All these significant ornamental lines were likewise adorned with their proper colours, adding a grace and richness to the architecture that it is impossible to conceive without having seen. Stretching from the abacus of one column to the other in the direction of the avenue is one of the two architrave stones. Its length is twenty-five feet; its width, five; and depth, ten feet. The curved form of the under surface is the effect of accident or violence. The roof-stones that stretched across the central avenue resting on these architrave blocks, must have measured more than thirty feet, but none of these are *in situ*. How these immense blocks were raised seventy feet above the floor of the temple, we have no conception, for in none of the blocks is there any trace of the means employed to raise them, such as lewis holes or semicircular furrows, as there are in the blocks of the temples of Greece and Sicily.

J. B.

NOTE.—The late Mr. Robert Stephenson, the eminent engineer, who had been much in Egypt, was of opinion that the stones of these temples were moved on rollers, up inclined planes of sand, and thus placed in their proper

XXXV.—TEMPLE OF KARNAK.

places; and that the temple, when its top-stones were being placed, was in appearance one vast sand-heap. As soon as the last stone was in its place, the sand was removed, and there appeared to the world a finished building needing only the sculptured details, which were then first drawn, and afterwards cut upon the walls.

S. S.

A king, from the architrave stone of a temple, hastening to the sacrifice.

PLATE XXXVI.

Temple of Karnak. — Columns with Capitals in Imitation of Papyrus Bud.

THIS is a view on the north side of the centre, the observer standing in the seventh transverse avenue and looking westward. Here again we see how the former consistent decoration of those bud-shaped capitals has been defaced, as the architect would esteem it, with the legends and names of Rameses IV. (See fig. 31). To the historian, however, this substitution of the names and titles of a king who, but for this repetition, would have been unknown, is highly valuable, as it fills up a space in the history of the country, which otherwise must have been left to conjecture or entirely unknown. And this substitution of names and titles for ornament, however appropriate if already known, is far less damaging to the interests of either study, than that of obliterating one king's name for the insertion of another, as before noticed in some of the buildings in Western Thebes, and on the obelisk of Thothmes on this side of the Nile.

J. B.

PLATE XXXVII.

The fallen Obelisk, and the Obelisk of Thothmosis ii. at Karnak.

THIS is a view looking northwards, the spectator standing at the south end of the court of the large obelisks. The upper part of the southern obelisk lies on the ground, with its apex towards the spectator. By whom and when this extraordinary work of art was thrown down and broken into fragments is entirely unknown. From this fragment, Mr. Robert Hay procured the mould out of which the cast on the staircase of the British Museum was made; and there it may be seen, as well as in this beautiful photograph, that the figure of Amun on the apex has been inserted in the place of a former divinity, who likewise wore a cap decorated with long feathers: for if the former figure had not been habited in a similar head-dress to the present, there would have been no necessity for lowering the surface of the granite so much above the head of the figure. The same obliterations and reinsertions occur on the standing obelisk, as may be easily discerned on the spot with an opera-glass—but so skilfully executed that they escaped the observation of Rosellini and Champollion, who have published the inscriptions on its four sides without suspecting that there had been any change. Nor was it ascertained, till the cast which is now in the British Museum was made; and it yet remains to be found out when and on what occasion these particular defacements were done, and when and on what occasion the reinsertions, as they now appear, were made.

One circumstance respecting these changes, as far as regards these particular monuments, is, that it is certain that both obelisks were standing on their pedestals, as the northernmost is at this moment; and therefore a

XXXVII.—FALLEN OBELISK, AND THE OBELISK OF THOTHMOSIS II.

scaffolding reaching to the very apex (see fig. 40) must have been erected, both for the purpose of the obliteration and for the reinsertion; and consequently it would be unreasonable to conclude—especially when we take into consideration that the names of the same divinities, whenever they are found on monuments anterior and of the age of these obelisks, have likewise been obliterated and reinserted—that the occasions were occasions of small importance; and we should look in vain, in the history of the country, for events of sufficient religious or political weight, if we except the invasion and expulsion of the Hiksos, the seven years of plenty and famine in the time of the Son of Israel, or the circumstances attending the Exodus. Which or how many of these important events, recorded in the histories of the country, are connected with these signficant marks on the monuments remains yet to be reasoned out, for hitherto the monuments have not been critically examined with a view to the elucidation of this curious subject. It may be mentioned, that obliterations and insertions of the names of the same divinities occur on the obelisk in the Piazza St. Giovanni Laterano in Rome. One other remark in connection with this curious inquiry which is illustrated by the two beautiful statues of lions in our national collection brought from Ethiopia by the present Duke of Northumberland, and that is, the inscriptions on the plinth exhibit the obliterations, but not the subsequent insertions; whether because during the interval these statues were taken to Ethiopia and thus escaped the consequence of the subsequent event, is not known. To the left is a row of ten Osiride figures; these statues seem to have at one time supported the roof of a portico surrounding the court and at some subsequent period built into the wall, and a row of columns substituted in their stead.

Fig. 40.

XXXVII.—FALLEN OBELISK, AND THE OBELISK OF THOTHMOSIS II.

The dilapidations in this part of the ruins of Karnak are so great that it has hitherto been impossible, and still is without making extensive and well directed excavations, to explain either the former or latter plan. Much light might be thrown on the circumstances attending the changes in the religious opinions as well as the architectural contrivances with which they were possibly connected.

J. B.

Supposed restoration of the great Sphinx.

PLATE XXXVIII.

Side View of the Obelisk at Karnak.

So beautifully distinct is this photograph, that we here see some of the alterations described by Mr. Bonomi on the last Plate. The head-dress of the god Amun-ra may be seen to be cut on a hollowed surface below the face of the stone; both on the small pyramid at the top of the obelisk, and again on the left-hand column of sculpture below the pyramid. Though the casts from this sculpture, on the landing-place in the British Museum, are of the size of the originals, yet for want of a good light, this curious alteration, which is of historic importance, cannot be there seen so easily as in our photograph. The large hawk which stands at the head of the middle row of sculpture is the word Pharaoh, or rather the word Ouro, *king;* which with the Coptic article prefixed becomes Pa-ouro, *the king:* the well-known title of the Egyptian sovereigns, so often used in the Bible.

S. S.

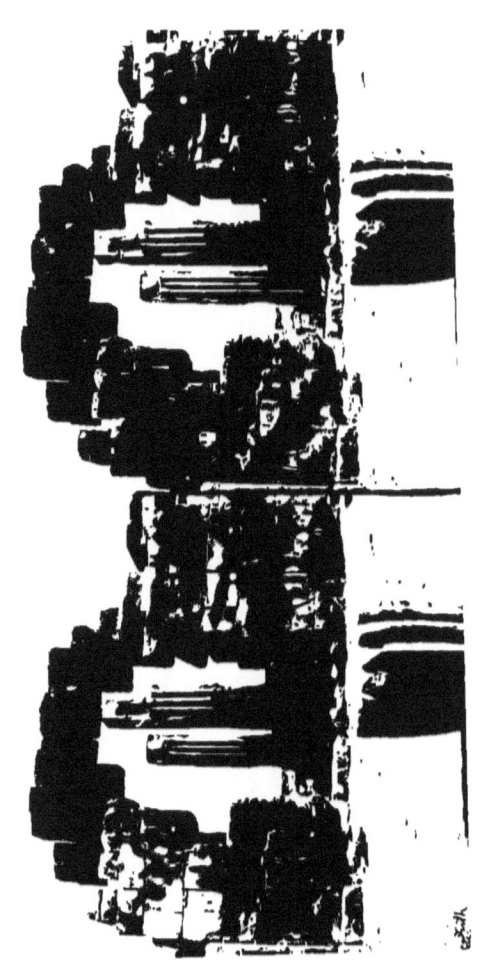

PLATE XXXIX.

Karnak.

This is a view of those two square granite blocks that stand in the small court before the granite sanctuary; and of which we have already seen the east faces in view, Plate XXIX. As was before stated, that block, to the south or right-hand of the entrance to the granite sanctuary, was decorated with figures of the papyrus or flower of the south; and the block, to the north or left-hand of the entrance, with the papyrus or flower of the north. It follows, then, as the figures of the papyrus of the south are sculptured on the block nearest to the spectator, that he is looking northwards. The capitals of the columns of the Ptolemaic and Roman temples of Egypt are mostly composed of a combination of these two flowers; and usually with a third, representing the bud of the ordinary or northern papyrus. These two gracefully adorned monoliths are about 20 feet high. As before stated, the two surfaces at right angles with those seen in this view are divided into compartments, in which is represented Thothmosis III. being received by the divinities of the temples comprised in these ruins of Karnak. From somewhere in this vicinity was brought that monolith in the British Museum. It is a remarkable instance, which may be seen and studied with all convenience, of that change in the religious opinions of the ancient Egyptians so frequently alluded to. It represents the same Pharaoh as that on the monoliths of the photograph, being conducted into the temple by two divinities, Mandoo-ra and Athor; but as this subject is repeated on both sides of the block of granite, it forms a group of six figures. It will be observed, on examining this work, that the figures of the divinities are in a different style of sculpture, and in lower relief than the figures of the king; and this is because the original divinities had been violently broken at the time of their falling into discredit, and subsequently re-carved

XXXIX.—KARNAK.

out of what was left, supplying portions (which were attached by cramps to the shoulders of the two male figures) when these divinities were again restored to public favour.

The opening in the wall through which the view of the granite blocks is obtained was made by violence, and it is almost miraculous that the two courses of stones above the opening should not yet have fallen; for to nothing else but the accidental lateral pressure of the blocks can their present position be attributed. The surface of the wall is covered with beautifully executed Egyptian bassi-rilievi representing the king making offering to various divinities. To the right is a piece of the wall of the granite sanctuary, and the ends of the sandstone blocks that form an upper roof for that building.

It should be mentioned that the defacement in the lower part of the southern or nearer monolith is occasioned by the corrosive nature of the nitrous earth in which it had been buried for so many ages, and which has only lately been removed by M. Mariette.

Quite in the foreground is the lower part of a column composed of a greater number of papyrus stalks than is usual, and of which there is no perfect example now extant. At the base of these stalks can be discerned those close-fitting leaves that grow at the base of the natural plant. To understand the view, we refer the student to the plan.

J. B.

NOTE.—Upon the altar, or monolith, described above by Mr. Bonomi, in the British Museum, it would seem as if the figure once standing beside the king had been the god Amun-ra, the great god of Thebes; whose name and figure had been changed, at some time when art had very much declined in excellence, into Mandoo-ra, a god worshipped chiefly in the Delta, though not exclusively. When this religious change was made upon the several monuments, is doubtful. It may indeed have been made so soon, that the second change of replacing the name of Amun-ra upon some of them may have been, as Mr. Bonomi supposes, the work of Rameses II. But the very bad style of workmanship with which the figure of Mandoo-ra has been cut, leads me to think it was done much later. I would conjecture that Amun-ra was set aside to make way for Mandoo-ra, when the kings of Mendes were masters of Egypt, about B.C. 400; and that the second change of giving again to Amun-ra his own honours, was not made till the time of the Greek kings, the Ptolemies, when the sanctuary of Karnak was repaired. The figure of one of the two goddesses has also been cut down with those of the god, and it helps us to put a date upon the alterations here made. The three new and rude figures have not got the flat stomach of the early Egyptian statues; and in this respect, while they show a bad style of art, they show a better knowledge of the human figure. This, also, would lead us to think that the new figures were cut after the fall of Thebes.

S. S.

PLATE XL.

The Temple of Erment or Hermonthis.

THESE ruins are situated on the west bank of the river, about ten miles south of Thebes. The columns of this temple, like those of Esne, Edfu, and other temples of the latter Greek and Roman kings of Egypt, are of a more slender proportion than those of the temples built by the Pharaohs or native kings. The capitals of these columns are of the composite varieties frequently found in the buildings of this epoch, and of exceedingly excellent workmanship. In the Lower Empire, this temple was converted into a Christian church of great importance, as may be judged from the remains; and there is still here, and in the neighbouring villages, a considerable Christian population. And here may be observed a little nicety, well exhibited in the photograph, respecting the form of the stalks which descend from the different flowers of which the capital is formed. Those which proceed from the buds and the expanded papyrus are nearly round, while those which proceed from the flower resembling that on the granite block on the south of the sanctuary of Karnak are angular. On the shaft of the nearest column is a figure of the celebrated beauty and queen, Cleopatra, making an offering to one of the divinities of the temple; and on the second column is that of her son, Cæsarion, making an offering to the bull-headed divinity, Basis, to whom, with Mandoo, this temple seems to have been dedicated. The hieroglyphical decorations have suffered very much from wilful defacement. There is much still to be learned from these Græco-Egyptian temples, respecting the mythology of the Egyptians, considerably modified in the style of the inscriptions and figures that appear on the walls of temples of this and the Roman period, from that of the ancient Pharaohism.

XL.—THE TEMPLE OF ERMENT OR HERMONTHIS.

Between the temple and the Nile is an artificial lake lined with masonry, in which the waters of the inundation are still retained for some time after they have left the surrounding fields. This lake so much resembles a libation-stone in the British Museum, that it might be taken for a small model of the artificial lake or tank of Hermonthis, that we have given it in the margin (see fig. 41). The four flights of steps preceding, as in the model, existed in the time of Denon, as may be verified by his sketch; but, of late years, so much stone has been carried away from these ruins for the construction of factories, that the likeness to the ancient model is now hardly traceable.

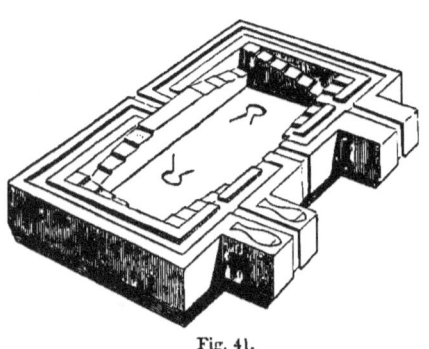

Fig. 41.

In a similar lake to this were kept the tame crocodiles at Dendera.

J. B.

Note.—Mandoo, the god of this temple, would seem to have belonged, originally, to Lower Egypt, though not unknown in Thebes in the time of Rameses II. But it is only in the later days that we find temples built for his worship in the upper country. We have already seen, in examining Queen Nitocris's obelisk at Karnak, that, when Thebes fell from its high rank, Mandoo-ra usurped the place of Amun-ra, on some of the monuments of that once proud city; and that afterwards, under the first Ptolemies, the priests of Thebes were allowed to displace Mandoo-ra, and give back to Amun-ra his own honours. Now, in the reign of Cleopatra, in the year B.C. 40, we find from this temple that his worship, driven out of Thebes, had settled here at Hermonthis, eight miles higher up the river.

XL.—THE TEMPLE OF ERMENT OR HERMONTHIS.

Cleopatra's elder brother and colleague on the throne was drowned in the year B.C. 47; her younger brother and second colleague was murdered in the year B.C. 44. As this temple is dedicated in the name of the queen and her son, Cæsarion, the child of Julius Cæsar, it must have been finished after the death of both her brothers. Fig. 42 contains the names of the queen and her son, spelt Kleopatras and Caisaros, both words being in the Greek genitive case.

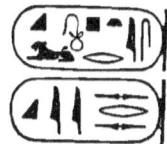

Fig. 42.

S. S.

PART OF THE TEMPLE OF KOUM OMBOS

PLATE XLI.

Part of the Temple of Koum Ombos.

THIS is a view looking south, of part of one of the towers of the gateway which led to the temples of Ombos. These ruins are situated on the east bank of the Nile, and are called by the Arabs Komombo, having added to the original word the epithet *kom*, hill; as in fact it is, the sand from the desert having invaded the locality, and buried the temple nearly to its roof. Here it may be said that we have entered the sandstone formation, of which the sand now encumbering this ruin is the débris. Added to this catastrophe the Nile is making daily inroads on this eastern bank, and has already, by undermining the soil, hurled down the other tower of this gateway; and is gradually burying beneath its waves a small temple which, a few years ago, stood near the shore, in almost its primitive beauty, rich in coloured sculpture of the Ptolemaic period. The stream is excessively rapid at this spot, especially during the inundation, so that no boat can be moored close to the ruin: and agreeably to the law of rivers, this bank presents a steep ascent, while the opposite coast is flat and shelving. Indeed an island is in the course of formation on the opposite coast, the shore of which is rich in small fragments of brick and pottery; showing the violent action of the current on the bank above Ombos, and prognosticating the entire submersion of the whole of these ancient buildings at no distant period. The block of masonry before us appears to be part of the inside surface of the tower, to the left hand of the gate. A series of square holes have been cut in it for the insertion of beams of wood, after the temple ceased to be regarded sacred, and became the abode of Christian monks. The figure of Ptolemy Auletes is three times repeated; in the upper compartment offering to Amun and possibly Isis; in the second, to Aroeris and Isis; in the third, to Isis and Pthah.

XLI.—PART OF THE TEMPLE OF KOUM OMBOS.

The very black shadow proceeding from the tower is not owing entirely to the absence of light, but partly to the colour of the material on which the shadow falls, it being the remains of a crude brick wall made of the dark earth of Egypt. This wall beginning from the left-hand tower of this stone gateway encircled all the sacred buildings of Ombos, joining the tower on the right-hand of the gateway, whose stones form a confused mass sloping with a rapid inclination into the river. In this crude brick wall, of great thickness, is inserted a small stone gateway which belonged to the ancient temple, bearing the names of Thothmes III., and the queen who erected the large obelisks of Karnak. Rosellini gives a view of this gate, of sufficient size to make the hieroglyphics in the ovals, to any one who will take the trouble to compare, unmistakably the same as those in the ovals of those obelisks; and hence establishing the fact of the existence in this spot of a temple in the time of the Pharaohs, 1350 years before our era; and rebuilt again, about 1200 years afterwards, by the Ptolemy above mentioned.

J. B.

Note.—The figures in this photograph are large enough to show the style of the Egyptian artists under the Ptolemies when drawing the human figure, which was far removed from the simplicity which we observe in the older statues. In the female figures the dress is tight and transparent, meant to show the form; which here swells unnaturally, with an affectation of grace and beauty, which is much less pleasing than the straight stiffness of the old statues. The god Pthah is, as usual, swaddled like a mummy. The king's apron or petticoat is held out by a wooden frame, like the hoops now worn by ladies. This frame is seen, yet more clearly, in the statues in the British Museum.

This temple of Ombos was begun by Ptolemy Philometor, and finished by this king Ptolemy Auletes. See his name, fig. 23.

S. S.

PLATE XLII.

The Temple of Koum Ombos.

ADVANCING a few steps farther up the sandy slope, we shall arrive at this view of the principal temple, which, as we perceive, is buried up to the stone in which the pivots of the gates were inserted. This portico is remarkable for being divided by a central column into two entrances; and accordingly we see two winged globes, one over each gate, the column at the right being that sustaining the two central architrave stones. To have placed a column in the centre of a portico, giving access but to one shrine, would have been an architectural inconsistency of which no Egyptian architect would have been guilty; and we find that this portico gave access to two separate shrines: in one, Savak, the crocodile-headed divinity, was worshipped; and in the other, Aroeris, the hawk-headed god; the former being, as it would appear, the more important—the inhabitants of Ombos worshipping the crocodile, on the principle that the Chinese worship the god of evil, to implore him to avert calamities of which he himself is the author; and there is a curious story preserved in a Latin author of the deadly contest between the people of this place and Tentyris or Dendera, who entertained a different opinion respecting the crocodile-headed divinity. This contest between the people of the different cities and nomes, seems to have been alluded to in Isaiah (chap. xix. v. 2), in which chapter also is hinted the entire disappearance of the papyrus plant, so important, and, as we may judge, so esteemed a production. On the architrave stone, resting on the front column and the one immediately behind it, may be seen the crocodile-headed divinity sitting between two hawks with extended wings.

In the foreground are some fine blocks of stone, fallen at no distant period. Those two hiding the shaft of the column, and near to which the

XLII.—THE TEMPLE OF KOUM OMBOS.

standing figure of an Arab boatman affords some idea of their dimensions, are the architrave and cornice stones that rested on that column and its companion on this side. Still more in the foreground is another enormous block, forming the cornice or curvetto moulding of the next architrave. Of the dimensions of this block the man sitting gives a good notion.

This block is decorated with the three stripes likened to the triglyphs of a Greek temple, and between each triglyph the ovals containing the name and titles of Ptolemy Philometor, by whom this double shrine was begun, and continued by his successors Physcon and Auletes. On the flat surface of the top of the curvetto is a Greek inscription, of which the translation is, "For the good of the King Ptolemy and Queen Cleopatra, his sister; gods Philometores, and their children; the infantry, cavalry, and the others, in the Ombite nome; this temple has been erected to the great god Aroeris Apollo, and to the con-templar gods for their benevolence towards them."

J. B.

Note.—Fig. 43 is the first name of King Ptolemy Philometor. It may be translated, "Son of the two gods Epiphanes, approved by Pthah and Horus, like Ra and Amun."

S. S.

Fig. 43.

PLATE XLIII.

The Temple of Koum Ombos.—The Portico.

This view affords a good notion of the elaborate form of the Egyptian capital of the column to the left of the entrance of the shrine of Savak, the crocodile-headed god of Ombos. Precisely the same form of capital occurs again on the right of the entrance to the shrine of Aroeris, the hawk-headed god. Complicated as this variety may appear, it will be found to be constructed with a common-sense consistency that a single diagram can render intelligible. It is composed of the flowers of a water-plant (see figs. 44 and 45), bound together round a common centre in five tiers, according to the order of their growth. The first tier consists of four large, full-grown specimens. The second, of eight; the third, of sixteen; the fourth, of thirty-two; the fifth, of sixty-four. Each flower sends down its own particular stalk to be bound by five horizontal bands. When this capital is found in a perfect condition with its various colours, the design appears less complicated and the beauty of the composition greatly enhanced. No colour, however, remains on any of the capitals, for the temple was never entirely finished, as here and there in the soffits may be seen the squares that had been ruled for drawing out the work to be sculptured.

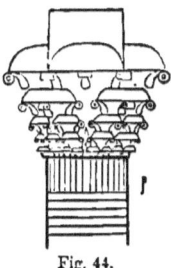

Fig. 44.

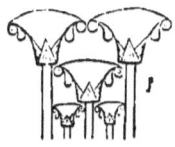

Fig. 45.

In the foreground are the two enormous blocks that formed the architrave and cornice that rested partly on that column and its companion, to the left of which there are no remains above the sand. These two blocks are the same as those that obstruct the view of this

XLIII.—THE TEMPLE OF KOUM OMBOS—THE PORTICO.

column in the last photograph. The row of holes at the base of the stone forming the curvetto were probably for the insertion of beams. The ornament on the torus, and the hieroglyphics on the frieze, are well rendered. And here may be remarked the different proportion that these members of the entablature bear to each other when compared with the Pharaohnic temple of Medinet-Habou. The two figures enable the mind to form some idea of the stupendous masonry of this temple.

J. B.

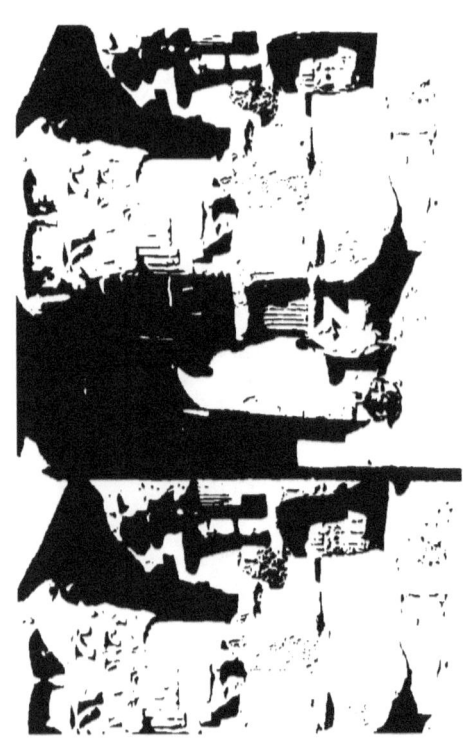

PLATE XLIV.

Columns at Koum Ombos, with Composite Capitals.

THIS is a view of the central column of the double entrance; and that massive construction buried in the sand nearly up to where the pivots were inserted, sustained the weighty bronze valves of both entrances. This capital is composed of the same water-plant as its two companions, but there are only four tiers; and consequently sixty-four flowers and stalks fewer than in the capitals on each side. The single square block that fitted into that rectangular space, and completed the curvetto moulding, has been wantonly thrown down. The photograph gives an accurate delineation of the rough surface to which it adhered. The column behind has a capital composed of two varieties of the papyrus and the buds of the plant, altogether of a much more complicated structure than the two already described, which we may have an opportunity of explaining if we should meet with an example less obscured.

Between the central and the two columns to the right appears a little piece of the crude brick wall that surrounded the sacred buildings of Ombos, to which the pylon, now half fallen into the river, gave access.

J. B.

PLATE XLV.

Fallen Architrave of Koum Ombos.

This is a view looking northwards. The nearest column is in the second row of this portico. Its capital represents a single fully expanded papyrus: but it has not that graceful, elegant contour of those specimens of this ancient order in the central avenue of Karnak. Near to this column can be seen a portion of the capital of one of the columns of the third row, which is again of another variety of the composite order.

In the foreground we have a mass of stone, part of the architrave of a nearer column; and a little farther the cornice belonging to the entablature of the column to the left.

Under it are sitting the captain and two sailors, their faces, as usual, as much as possible, turned away from the camera, because their likenesses should not be known to the Angel Gabriel, in order that, at the day of judgment, he should not say to them, "This is your image, and this is your image, and this likewise. Divided, therefore, be your soul into as many pieces, to animate these images; and be content with what is left for your share."

J. B.

Note.—On the cornice, beside the name of Ptolemy Auletes, is that of his daughter Cleopatra Tryphæna, who for one year, B.C. 57, governed Egypt as queen, while her father, who had fled to Rome from his offended subjects, was begging the senate for an army to replace him on the throne.

S. S.

PLATE XLVI.

Columns at Koum Ombos with Capitals of full-blown Papyrus.

THE nearest column, immediately in the foreground, against which the captain and a sailor, more bold than the rest, are sitting, has a capital imitating the palm. The next is the papyrus capital described in the last, on the shaft of which, guarded by two *uræi*, or sacred asps, is the oval containing the name of Ptolemy Neus Dionysus. It occurs just over the head of a man who entertains a superstitious reverence or dread respecting the commonly received legend about the day of judgment, and has therefore turned his back to the camera. There most likely has been a conversation respecting the matter, some subtlety of argument produced, as to how much the sun is implicated, which has emboldened some and terrified others. Behind this column is that to the right of the entrance to the shrine of Aroeris.

J. B.

NOTE.—The oval containing the king's name on both these columns is upheld by two asps, or sacred serpents, of the cobra capella species. This animal has the power of raising its ribs, and swelling its chest, as here represented. Its fore part stands upright from the ground; the loose skin about its head gives to it the appearance of a crown, and hence its name, basilisk, or *uræus*, meaning the *royal serpent*. This, with the Egyptians, was the serpent of good, and must be distinguished from the serpent

XLVI.—COLUMNS AT KOUM OMBOS.

of evil, with which it is often placed in opposition. In the upper row of sculptures on the second column, the king's name alternates with the figure of a man sitting on one heel, and holding in each hand a notched stick or palm branch, which is the hieroglyphic for the "year." By this the king was entitled, "Lord of the years."

S. S.

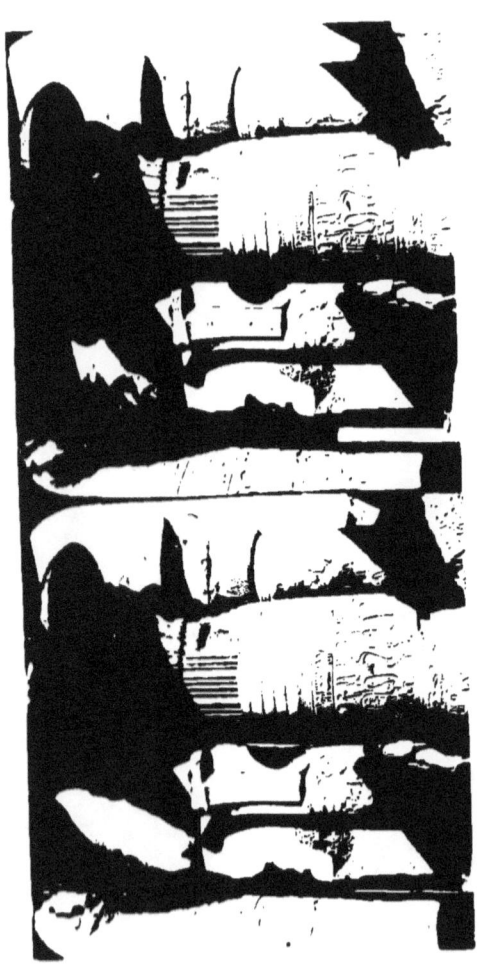

PLATE XLVII.

Columns at Koum Ombos with Palm-leaf Capitals.

VIEW from within the portico looking southwards. The most distant column is that which was the most near in the last picture, namely, the palm capital (see fig. 46). Rembrandt himself could not have desired a more effective piece of chiaro-scuro than this beautiful photograph displays. In the extreme distance is a piece of the brick wall, and picturesquely posed against the fine column is an Arab lad, who takes care not to look at the camera. This capital, which is of a rare ancient type, is amusingly divided into nine branches, each face being 40° of the circle. See fig. 47. The elements of which this capital is constructed are those of fig. 48.

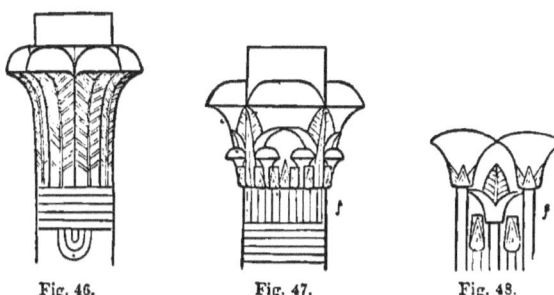

Fig. 46.   Fig. 47.   Fig. 48.

Then we have the papyrus capital, and between the two, the column behind the one which supports the entablature of the entrance to the shrine of the hawk-headed god. This capital is formed of two different plants and buds arranged in five tiers, viz., four papyri fully expanded; then four of the plant of Upper Egypt; then eight lesser fully expanded papyri; then sixteen lesser of Upper Egypt; and lastly, thirty-two buds.

J. B.

PLATE XLVIII.

View through the Portico at Koum Ombos.

THIS is a view looking southwards down the second avenue, or between the second and third row of columns. To the left is the wall at the back of the portico, in which are the entrances to the two shrines. This wall is surmounted by the usual curvetto; but above that is a row of serpents with disks on their heads. It is on this wall that the Greek inscription already quoted is engraved. There is a good sample of this decoration, representing serpents looking over the wall to guard the sacred edifice, in the Crystal Palace, and also in the British Museum, in one of those blocks of basalt forming the intercolumnar wall of the monolith temple, mentioned by Herodotus, at Sais, which has been engraved (see fig. 49), as giving a very tolerable general notion of the façade of an

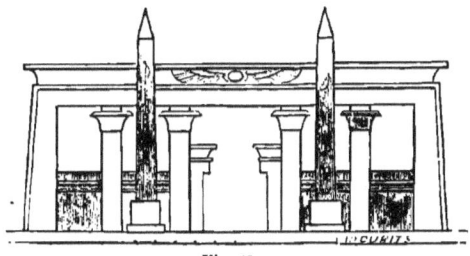

Fig. 49.

Egyptian temple, and one of which it is shrewdly conjectured we have so many fragments in our own national repository.

The last row of columns have capitals of a construction of which there are no other examples extant, not composed of the usual elements, nor so consistently combined.

J. B.

XLVIII.—VIEW THROUGH THE PORTICO AT KOUM OMBOS.

NOTE.—Our woodcut will explain the form of the portico in most of the Egyptian temples. The roof is flat, the outside of the wall slopes slightly backwards like the side of a hill, the inside of the wall is upright. This gives a great appearance of strength; the columns are four, six, or eight in number, according to its size. In front of it stand two obelisks, or stone needles. Originally the space between the columns was open, so that everybody could see the ceremonies which took place under the portico. This is the form of the temple at Rebek; but afterwards, in order to mark the separation between the priests and the laity, a low wall was raised, so as to block up every intercolumnar space except the middle one; and that was closed by a door. Thus the public was shut out from a sight of what was passing within. These intercolumnar walls are always ornamented with the same class of sculptures; so much so, that of two small slabs in basalt in the British Museum, we are able to pronounce that they are intercolumnar walls of a small temple, or model of a temple, twelve feet high. Further, in one of the museums of Rome there is a third slab of the same size, and with the same sculpture, which no doubt belonged to the same little temple. We have also in the British Museum two small obelisks of basalt, which might have stood in front of it, and the capital of a column of the same stone. By the help of these stones we are able to reconstruct our temple as seen in the woodcut. The darker portions show the stones which we possess, the lighter portions are drawn by analogy from other temples. And having thus reconstructed it, we are enabled to say, that this is the very temple described by Herodotus as the wonderful monolith temple of Sais; not indeed, of a single block of stone, but having every part one single block. The lighter parts of our woodcut, being the stones not known to be in the museums of Europe, are no doubt safe buried under the mounds of Sais, awaiting the enterprise of some travellers to dig them up—under mounds which give to the ruins of that city the name of Sa-el-hager, or Sais the stony.

S. S.

PLATE XLIX.

General View of Koum Ombos.

THIS view is taken from the hill of sand at the back of the temple, looking directly across the Nile towards the west. How deceived were the Greek kings in the choice of the locality for this magnificent work; and how deceived would the chronologist be who should found any arrangement on the antiquity of the earth, or the antiquity of the building, from data furnished by the condition of this temple. Undermined from the west by the approach of the river, and buried from the east by the encroachment of the sand of the Arabian desert, this landmark of history, this witness of the greatness and wealth of the Ptolemies, will, at no distant time, entirely disappear. Twenty years is usually as nothing in the silent geological changes that are going on; but in this spot it counts as much as twenty hundreds in others. A similar geological change is taking place, but with less rapidity, in another ancient locality, but seldom visited by travellers because of the distance from the bank of the river; and this is at a place north of Thebes, called by the natives Araba-el-Medfuna. In this instance it is the Libyan desert which has advanced and buried to the roof an ancient temple built by the father of Rameses II; and here the river, instead of acting in concert with the land, has apparently receded and left a considerable territory of productive soil. The ancient buildings and tombs in that locality are the most intact of any in Egypt, from the circumstance of their being buried, and that in very ancient times: so remarkable is the aspect of the place and the fact of the complete burial of the ancient structure, that it has obtained the epithet el-Medfuna, *the buried*. The largest temple as yet discovered in this capital of the Thinite Nome, possesses a feature not known in any other now existing, and that is a row of arches built of approaching stones, possibly intended to be imitated by the son and successor

XLIX.—GENERAL VIEW OF KOUM OMBOS.

of this Pharaoh in the brick constructions surrounding the Memnonium, possessed by no other temple, if we except only the crude brick arch attached to the small temple called Dayr-el-Medinet.

In the foreground, near the two sitting figures, may be remarked the finely delineated undulatory surface of the sand, as effected by the almost constant strong north wind which blows for nine months down the valley of the Nile from the Mediterranean; and how, at the north side of the temple, the sand is scooped out and carried to the south side; and yet how surely and gradually the whole is being buried, but, perhaps, not before the Nile will have thrown down the remaining tower of the gateway to the left of the picture, and menaced the portico of the temple. We may notice the footprints in the sand as distinct from the wave-like effect of the wind, and how much more numerous the footprints are on the south side of the temple than on the north, because it is in that direction that the boat of the explorer is moored: the velocity of the stream rendering it impossible to secure the boat anywhere near the temple, except just above, where the stream impinges with such violence against the bank. We will notice, also, how carefully the Arab turns his back to the camera, instructed by the universally accepted Mohammedan legend before alluded to.

J. B.

PLATE L.

Sandstone Quarries at Hager Silsilis.

GENERAL view of the quarries of Hager Silsilis, looking southward. At this part of Egypt the valley of the Nile is so narrowed as to admit of little or no cultivation; for both banks are formed of sandstone rocks, which every here and there advance into the river. The stone of these quarries is of a remarkably regular formation. In one part, on this western bank, are some extensive excavations, chambers and chapels for the workmen, as well as tablets of great historical and religious interest. The name of the place is derived from a Coptic word signifying a chain, which happens to resemble the Arabic word for the same thing. It is to this circumstance that a tradition has grown up, and is well supported in the imagination of the Arabs by a remarkable piece of rock that resembles a nail-head or a colossal mushroom. To this rock, say the Arab boatmen, was attached a chain, which was stretched across the river by Pharaoh to prevent the boats passing that were laden with corn for the faithful in Lower Egypt. This remarkable piece of rock has acquired this mushroom form by having been so cut by the quarrymen, who left it standing in the middle of the quarry, bearing the original surface of the hill, and thus serving as an index of the extent of their labours.

In this view, the winding river and distant banks are charmingly represented.

J. B.

L.—SANDSTONE QUARRIES AT HAGER SILSILIS.

Note.—The range of mountains which press upon the river at Silsilis were probably the boundary between the little kingdoms of Thebes and Elephantine, before the whole of Upper Egypt fell under the more powerful sceptre of Thebes. This union took place about B.C. 1450, one hundred years before Lower Egypt fell and the two countries became one kingdom.

S. S.

The full-blown Papyrus.

PLATE LI.

Sandstone Quarries at Hager Silsilis—General View.

THE vast quantities of stone that have been taken out of this quarry may be estimated by the proportion the figures bear to the cuttings near to which they stand; and the beautiful quality of the stone, by the smoothness of the surface and the sharpness of the angles.

J. B.

NOTE.—The quarries of Silsilis gave to the Egyptians the best building-stone in the country, or, at least, in the upper country. All the chief temples of the Thebaid, from Silsilis down the river till we come to the limestone in the neighbourhood of Memphis, were the produce of these quarries. The limestone of Thebes was not found to be so good for building purposes, and was less used.

S. S.

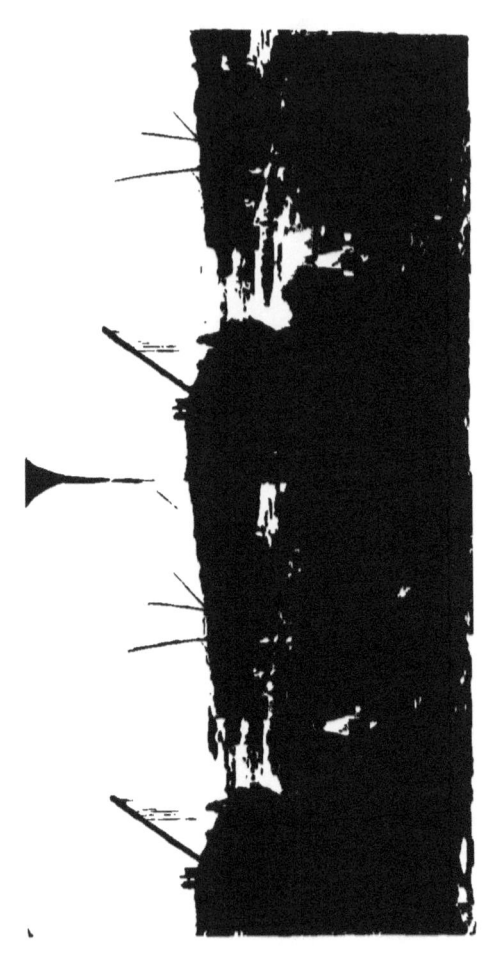

PLATE LII.

Assouan, or Syene.

THE beach of Assouan, the ancient Syene, the southern confine of Egypt, as intimated by the sentence, "From the tower (migdol) of Syene, even unto the border of Ethiopia."

To our right is the island of Elephantine; consequently we are looking southwards. In the same direction, to the left, is a remarkable cemetery of small chapels or cubas, and gravestones, with cuphic inscriptions; and still farther to the left the granite quarries, out of which were probably cut those masterpieces of art and engineering science, which in ancient and modern times have excited the wonder of all men of science. To the left is a ruined mosque and tomb, belonging to the ancient town, which is now deserted, having been visited by a terrible plague. On this island, a few years ago, stood a temple of Amunothph III., built of granite. This and the stones of one other temple were taken by the late Viceroy Ibrahim Pacha to build a residence on the banks of the Nile nearly opposite.

Two doorposts, of granite, belonging to an outer court, bore the name of Alexander. A flight of steps leading from the water's edge on this side the island served as a nilometer—there being likewise lines and hieroglyphics on the walls supporting the steps, recording extraordinary inundations. In the distance is a hill, on which are the remains of a Christian building, not seen in this view, called Cubbet-el-horver; and but a mile beyond that is the cataract. The whole of this beach is covered with the stream during the inundation, but in the season of the low Nile it becomes a convenient landing-place for the goods brought from the north and destined for Ethiopia; for from hence they are carried on the backs of camels three miles south to the other side of the cataract, when they are again put on board the same vessels, thus rendered lighter for the purpose of passing the rapids. All those vessels are probably only waiting for wind to pass the cataract into

LII.—ASSOUAN, OR SYENE.

Nubia; because if they were intended to go north they would have their masts taken down.

Here the Arabic language ceases, and an African dialect, called Lisan-el-barabra, begins; which again changes for another dialect a few miles south. Here Amanga is the word for water, as if derived from the word Amuu; and farther south Isigu, as if derived from the word Isis. Here the first day of the week is no longer Iōm-el-had, but Kiviaki, a word seemingly derived from the Greek. Farther south, beyond the second cataract, the Arabic language is spoken in great purity. And here, in a small village to the east, is a tribe called Davoui, of Ababde Arabs, among whom are many who speak the Bishareen language, the dialect of the tribes inhabiting the desert between the Red Sea and the Nile from this point to Abyssinia. These people are the Blemyes of some writers; and their countrymen, who live near the sea, the Troglody of Pliny. Not far from this spot there used to be a few stones with some hieroglyphics on them, in a date grove, said to be the remains of a temple in which there was a well in which the sun could be seen at midday during summer; and, as before mentioned, in the island opposite is a nilometer, wherein the rise of the Nile is marked by certain lines on the wall of a stone staircase. J. B.

Note.—The words quoted by Mr. Bonomi from Ezek. xxix. 10, would be better translated, "From Magdolus to Syene on the borders of Ethiopia." Syene is in latitude 24° 5′ 30″, and thus is fifteen miles to the north of the tropic. On the longest day of the year, at noon, the sun's centre is vertical over a spot fifteen miles to the south of Syene; hence at that moment the sun's northern edge is exactly over Syene; and Strabo informs us that there was an astronomical well in that city, down which the sun then shone without throwing any shadow. The astronomers were within one mile of the truth in regard to the latitude of the place, an exactness which we must in part set down to accident, as such accuracy is hardly to be looked for in observations made before the invention of the telescope. In the mosaic found at Preneste, in Italy, with a landscape view of the buildings of Egypt, this well is represented near the temple at Syene. S. S.

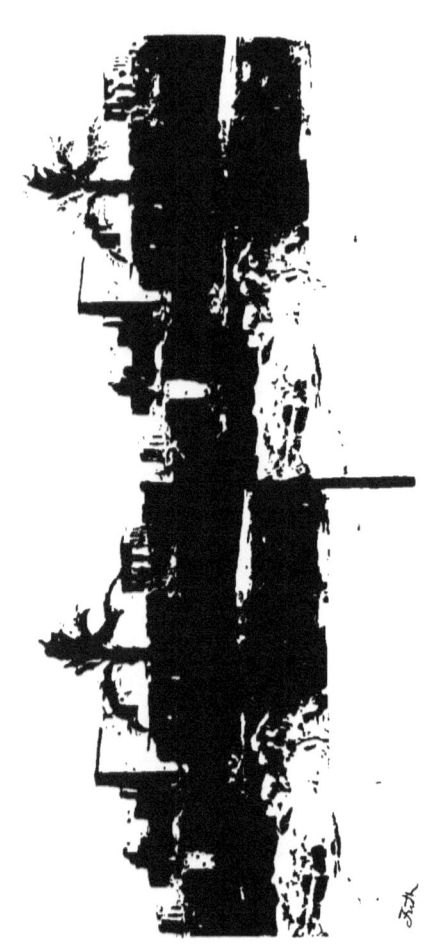

PLATE LIII.

The Temples on the Island of Philæ.

VIEW of the Island of Philæ from the Island of Biggeh. This is nearly the view you have of Philæ in approaching by the river from the north. The landing-place and staircase, it may be seen, is a little to the left beyond that projecting piece of wall. This gave access by the pylon on the left to the sacred enclosure, and thence to the courts of the temple, whose most sacred chambers are joined to the towers of the second gateway. The beautiful colonnade that connects the towers of the outer and inner gate belongs to a temple of Athor, almost in perfect condition; on its roof are the crude brick walls of chambers once inhabited by the Œconomos, or some important person belonging to the religious establishment located in this ancient building, as the crosses on the walls and the number of Christian Greek inscriptions, written on fragments of pottery and stone, sufficiently testify, if history had been silent on the subject.

This view is taken when the Nile is at its lowest, and the white line on the wall marks the usual limit of the inundation. The wall before us extends to the southern point of the island; it is the back of a continuous portico of columns, with a great variety of capitals, pleasing the eye and relieving the mind of that feeling of monotony so inherent in the ancient architecture of Greece and Italy. This wall is perforated with square openings, affording an extensive view of the cataract, and of the picturesque Island of Biggeh. Below the white line marking the extent of the rise of the waters, there are one or two doors leading down to the water by means of a staircase, which serves as a nilometer. Over the ruined part of the wall is a small hypæthral temple, which is situated on the other coast of the island, where the stream is both wide and rapid.

J. B.

LIII.—THE TEMPLES ON THE ISLAND OF PHILÆ.

NOTE.—Fig. 50 contains a view of these buildings nearly the same as our photograph, and accompanied with a ground-plan, which will enable us to understand the several following views. We see the very little regard

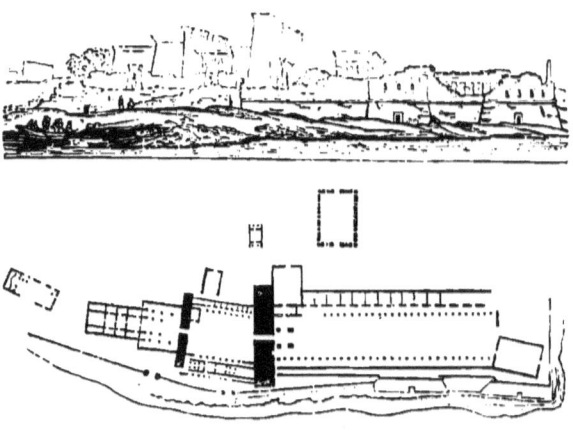

Fig. 50.

which the Egyptian architects had for regularity. When they enlarged the building with a new gateway, they made it, not parallel to the older and smaller gates, but set it crooked, so that it might make a suitable end to the new courtyard, which was by the bend of the river forced to take a new direction. In both of the courtyards we see the cells in which the priests dwelt as monks in solitude. It would seem that the priests in these pagan temples were the forerunners of the numerous Christian monks with which Egypt swarmed in the fourth and fifth centuries, and who taught monastic habits in Europe.

S. S.

PLATE LIV.

Temples on the Island of Philæ—Entrance.

HAVING landed and walked across the island, this view, turning towards the north of the two propyla belonging to the principal temple, will present itself. On the nearest tower to the right-hand side of the first gate is a colossal figure of Ptolemy Philadelphus, the founder (B.C. 260), making an offering to Horus and Isis, and again to Isis and Horus; between these last two figures is the square opening, out of which was thrust certain contrivances for retaining the staff of a flag-pole that was inserted into the groove below. The four smaller holes just over the top of the groove were made in after times for the beams of the roof of a chamber, occupied by the priests attached to the service of the church, when this ancient structure was converted into a Christian cathedral. Below these holes may be seen the crowns of the three divinities of the triad formerly worshipped in this temple, before whom Ptolemy, attired in the triple crown of Egypt, sacrifices the enemies of the country—represented by a group of foreigners, whose collected heads he is about to strike off with a single blow of the sacred falchion. The small oblong holes down the face of the tower, at the near end, give light to a staircase leading to chambers within it, the upper story being lighted by the three square holes in the curvetto. The same, or similar, sculptures are repeated on the surface of the tower on the other side of the entrance. The gate itself is decorated in the usual fashion with the winged disc and representations of the king bringing offerings to the gods. Before it stood two granite obelisks and two lions: one of the obelisks was brought to England by Belzoni. This gate leads into a square court, on the right-hand side of which is a portico belonging to the building we see in this

LIV.—TEMPLES ON THE ISLAND OF PHILÆ—ENTRANCE.

view, which is a suite of chambers with double roof; and on the left, a beautiful and nearly perfect temple, whose columns are seen in the View 55. The back of the court is formed by the gate and towers of the portico and more sacred chambers of the temple.

On the lower part of this second tower, seen in this view, we have Ptolemy, again of colossal dimensions, making offering to the two principal divinities of the temple, Horus and Isis; and above, the same king, the size of life, offering gifts to the particular triad of the district. In this tower, likewise, may be seen the square aperture and groove, as well as a series of holes for the timbers which supported the floors and roofs of chambers occupied by monks and priests, when the court immediately behind these towers was converted into a Christian church. This was done, as certain indications inform us, by stretching an awning over it, and making the portico serve as the altar chamber, which in the Greek and Coptic rites is separated from the laity by a decorated screen. To complete the arrangements, the heathen sculpture was covered with a coating of the mud of the Nile, which was plastered and painted with the figures of saints, and the Greek cross sculptured on all the door jambs.

In the foreground is an isolated gate, which formed a side entrance into the outer court, and was formerly joined to a colonnade. Still nearer are fragments of brick and stone, and the foundations of the walls of the houses of a once considerable Christian population.

J. B.

Fig. 51.

NOTE.—Ptolemy Philadelphus was the king under whom Egypt, as a Greek kingdom, rose to its greatest height. Fig. 51 is his name, which may be translated, "Beloved by Amun, to whom Ra gave victory." The peculiar head-dress here given to the king is the same as that given to a figure of the great Cyrus, on the wall of his palace in Persia, and used to denote his threat of making himself master of Egypt.

S. S.

PLATE LV.

Temples on the Island of Philæ.—The great Pylon.

THIS view, so beautiful in effect, is so nearly from the same point, that the traveller is already acquainted with all the important particulars connected with it. It presents, however, a view of the detached blocks of granite of which the island of Biggeh is formed, looking as if piled up by art—a circumstance which has suggested to the mind of the imaginative Arab an idle legend, that has taken root on the spot in a way that one could wish some physical truth had been planted. The story is this: Pharaoh caused those stones to be thrown into the Nile to prevent the stream flowing northwards, where Moses and the faithful were living; and a very remarkable pile, consisting of two or three rocks, looking something like an arm-chair, is said to be the seat he occupied while the work of throwing those blocks of granite into the stream, that now form the cataract, was being performed by the evil spirits in his employ. The people of these villages are all expert swimmers, even the women cross from rock to rock and island to island, balancing themselves on a log of dome or palm, using their hands as paddles, while they carry their goods on their heads. As there is not sufficient land for the cultivation of corn, they subsist, principally, on a few vegetables and fish, which the men catch in abundance at the subsidence of the inundation; some kind by diving at night, their companions in a boat holding a light: the divers grease themselves with castor-oil and mud, not to feel the cold. Other fish are caught by building out low walls inclosing a space into which they enter and cannot escape, when they are speared by the fishermen. The women make baskets of palm-leaves precisely like the ancient specimens in the museums of Europe. The men are likewise capital sailors and expert conductors of the boats across the rapids, for

LV.—TEMPLES ON THE ISLAND OF PHILÆ.—THE GREAT PYLON.

which they are paid a considerable fee. Having a language, never acquired by the natives on the north of Assouan, they possess advantages of no common order; and being, at the same time, very industrious and united, and possessing the faculty of imitation, readily acquire the Arabic.

J. B.

PLATE LVI.

Colonnade of the great Courtyard of the Temple of Philæ.

This is a view of part of the portico or colonnade on the right hand, in front of the first pylon. The doors are the entrances to small dark chambers, mostly encumbered with rubbish. The columns on this side of the court, like those on the opposite, are of a great variety of types.

J. B.

Fig. 52.

Note.—The doors in this view lead into the cells for the priests, seen in our woodcut, fig. 50, at plate 53. And we here add the drawing, from a statue in the British Museum, of one of these priests, who is supposed to be in holy meditation, and spending his life thus squatting on the ground in idleness (see fig. 52).

We further possess evidence that the Egyptian priests did live in confinement, under religious vows, in a curious document of which one half is in the Vatican and the other half in the British Museum. This is a papyrus roll, containing three petitions from a monk in the temple of Serapis, near Memphis, addressed to king Ptolemy Philometor, of which the first is dated in the year B.C. 157. He asks for a post in the army on behalf of his brother, which he hopes for as a favour due to himself for having lived fourteen years in religious confinement; and, for himself, he asks that he should be protected from the ill-treatment of the other religious persons in

LVI.—COLONNADE OF COURTYARD OF THE TEMPLE OF PHILÆ.

the same temple, who even pelt him through the window of his cell, in jealousy of him, because he was a Greek stranger and they were native Egyptians. In the later petitions, he reminds the king of his having presented the first to him through the window of his cell, on his visit to the temple.

S. S.

PLATE LVII.

The smaller Temple of Philæ.

CHARMING view, looking southwards, of the elegant ruin we saw at a distance over the dilapidated wall in the first picture of Philæ. This ruin is called by the natives the bed of Pharaoh, which idea must have been suggested by some European, because the beds of Egypt have no posts or cornice like those of Europe. It is an unfinished building, and never intended to have been hypæthral, or open to the sky; but whether it was intended that it should have had a chamber or cella within the peristyle, or that these columns should only have supported a roof, may be doubted. In either case the columns would necessarily be erected first, for there would not have been sufficient space for the machinery required to raise the blocks of stone of which the columns are composed if the walls of the cella had been built first.

The capitals of these columns are remarkable for the beauty and variety of the design, and the perfection of the execution. The abaci are higher than usual, except it was intended to engrave some design on them, of which there is no indication, and they are made of several blocks. In front of this building there is a terrace projecting into the river, the front wall of which is inclined and concave in plan, and very strongly bonded to the side walls by large blocks of stone. The intention of this construction is to obviate the natural tendency of the front wall to bulge outwards from the pressure of the earth, which during the inundation becomes saturated with moisture. This tendency is exhibited in the area walls of our London houses, and is supposed to be remedied by placing an iron from the foot of the centre rail against the front of the house, which usually results in breaking out the stone in which the rail is inserted,

LVII.—THE SMALLER TEMPLE OF PHILÆ.

or to the detriment of the house by pushing in the front wall. The hills which form the background are those of the eastern desert, which here approach the river. The trees in the foreground are good samples of the date-bearing palm, which produce a variety of the fruit much esteemed in Lower Egypt.

J. B.

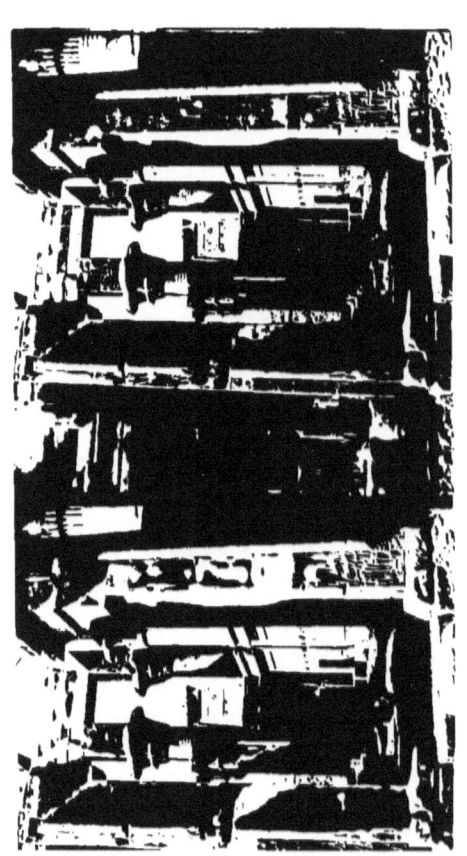

PLATE LVIII.

Entrance to the small Temple of Philæ.

THIS is a nearer view of the same temple from the terrace, and looking north or towards the island of Biggeh. There are no hieroglyphics, so that the precise date of the building cannot be known, nor are the architectural details below the capitals more than blocked out, probably as the stones came from the quarry. Between the column sustaining the door-post and the angle column at the opposite front, is a profile view of one of the towers of the gateway to the outer court of the great temple. The irregular furrows in the lower part of the wall of Pharaoh's bed are made by the inhabitants of the neighbouring villages, who come to this island to sharpen against these sandstone blocks the spears with which they fish and fight, and those little dagger-knives which every man wears in a neatly-made sheath strapped on the left arm.

There is hardly a lad of twelve or fourteen who does not know how to dress a sheep, rig a boat, tan leather, cook a variety of dishes, and make a handle for his knife.

J. B.

NOTE.—The style of the architecture, however, fixes the time of this building to the reigns of the later Ptolemies, after the larger temple was built by Philadelphus.

S. S.

PLATE LIX.

View from the Roof of the small Temple of Philæ.

This is a view, looking southward, taken from the roof of the colonnade leading up to the first gate from the south end of the island. The opposite colonnade terminates in a small chapel to Isis or Athor, before which stood two sandstone obelisks, one now only remaining. The walls on which this temple stands descend to the granite rocks which form this pointed end of the island. It was under this colonnade that we have already had a view of the entrances to the small chambers behind the wall to our left. The granite rocks that form the margin of the eastern desert are beautifully reflected in the calm stream. To the right we have the southern extremity of the island of Biggeh, with some remarkable granite boulders, as if placed there by man. Many of the more conspicuous blocks of granite have ancient inscriptions on them, the characters rendered conspicuous by the very simple process of picking away the polished blackened surface which the granite had acquired by great length of time, or some other agency; for no perceptible variation of tint can be recognized between the surface of the most ancient and most recent inscription.

J. B.

VIEW ON THE NILE. BOW FILES.

PLATE LX.

View of the Nile from Philæ.

A PEEP over the Nile from the island of Philæ, looking easterly. Those little specks on the opposite coast between the date-trees and the mast of the boat are people and goods that have arrived from Assouan, to be again embarked in the smooth water above the cataract. There is little or no cultivatable land between the Nile and those granite hills, except only the sloping banks of the river, which are diligently made to produce melons and other plants of the cucumber tribe, till the inundation returns. A ruined wall of crude brick peeps here and there above the sand all along the margin of the desert from Assouan to the foot of those hills, which is probably of Roman construction.

In the foreground we have the remains of terrace walls of well hewn stones. Moored to the bank is the commodious boat of the traveller, equipped for descending the stream, the principal mast and its lateen sail-yard lowered, the smaller one, called the "trinket," only kept up to be unfurled whenever a turn in the river and a slight variation of the wind from the almost constant northerly direction permits—giving the sailors a rest from rowing and tacking, and the traveller an agreable change from the rocking motion caused by the waves, which is sometimes sufficient to bring on the evils of a sea voyage.

J. B.

NOTE.—The Roman emperors entertained the gigantic plan of running a wall all round their large empire, wherever seas, or rivers, or mountains did not make it unnecessary. The wall which divided Scotland from England

LX.—VIEW OF THE NILE FROM PHILÆ.

was one part of that plan; and another part was this wall, which was to guard Egypt from the less civilized tribes in the south. This portion of the Roman *Limes* was probably built in the reign of Diocletian, when the general in command of Egypt found himself no longer strong enough to hold Nubia as part of the empire.

S. S.

PLATE LXI.

Ruins on the Island of Biggeh.

VIEW looking eastward of the two central columns of the portico of a temple built by Ptolemy Euergetes I., and finished in subsequent reigns, now standing on the south side of the island of Biggeh. This part of the ruin has been converted into an Arab dwelling by connecting the door-posts and intercolumnar walls with stones of all sizes and sorts, and protecting the roof of a chamber behind with acacia-bushes. The capitals of the columns are of that order before described, and the dwarf walls are crowned by the protecting uræus. On the pile of isolated granite blocks of which the whole island is composed, are the ruins of a Christian convent, beautifully situated, overlooking the island of Philæ.

J. B.

NOTE.—Fig. 53 is the name of Ptolemy Euergetes, the third of the family, and the most popular with the native Egyptians. He came to the throne in the year B.C. 246. His queen, Berenice, gave her name to the constellation called *Coma Berenices*.

S. S.

Fig. 53.

PLATE LXII.

Roman Arch on the Island of Biggeh.

THIS beautiful photograph is a view of the remains of the towers and gate of the temple, of which we saw the two central columns of the portico in the last picture. It is impossible to imagine a more happy combination of light and shadow, or a more picturesque or interesting view. The ancient rectangular gate was built by Ptolemy Euergetes I., on the site of a still older temple of Thothmes III. About the third century of our era, what was then left of this Ptolemaic restoration of the temple of Thothmes, was converted into a place of Christian worship, at which time the arch was inserted into the ancient gate in imitation of the Christian buildings of Rome and Constantinople; much, however, to the enfeeblement of the ancient entrance, which has subsequently suffered by the stones having been carried away for building purposes. In the distance are the granite mountains of the eastern desert; then the towers of the outer gate of the principal temple of Philæ, the little side entrance seen in View 55, and near to this a corner of the temple called the bed of Pharaoh; then the wall and the few date-trees that grow on this coast of the island of Philæ; and, lastly, the rude wall of loose stones of the present occupier of the ruin.

The particular angle at which the light falls on the face of the wall exhibits the sculpture to great advantage. On the lintel-stone we have the lower part of the figure of Ptolemy Euergetes I., twice repeated, standing and making offerings to three divinities. This, for the sake of uniformity, is again repeated on the other side of the centre. Each jamb is divided into four compartments, in which the same king would have been seen but for the encroachment of the arch, so many times offering various gifts to sixteen divinities, seven of whom are females. Below these religious sculptures we have two lines of hieroglyphics, and then a dado enriched with the papyrus plant under three forms of growth so often repeated and combined to form the capitals of the columns of this period.   J. B.

PLATE LXIII.

The Temple of Dabod in Nubia.

This view is taken from the first court, and looking westward. Dabod is situated on the west bank, and about ten miles south of Philæ. This temple is supposed to have been founded by an Ethiopian prince, but rebuilt by Ptolemy Philometor. Much of the sculpture on the walls also bears the name of the Roman emperor Tiberius, and much remains unfinished, the capitals being only blocked out.

In one of the dark rooms of the temple there used to be a kind of granite box or cupboard, which had evidently once had doors of wood or bronze. The names of Ptolemy Physcon and Cleopatra occurred in the inscription on it. The temple consists of three dark chambers, and a narrow staircase up to the roof, where there seems to have been contrived a tank over the central chamber, and a portico of columns.

In a line with the portico are still standing three gateways, two of which we see in the view, and the shadow of the third in the foreground. Each gate was joined to the great inclosing wall by the usual towers, forming three courts, the pavement of the last being four or five feet above the outer one. A wide terrace, the front wall of which is of massive construction, reaches to the river, and had a staircase leading up from the river. J. B.

Note.—Dabod is the town which has been usually thought to be the ancient Parembole, *the camp*, in the Roman Itinerary, where part of the Second Legion was stationed in the second and third centuries of our era. But the distances in the Itinerary are not laid down very correctly; and Dabod is five miles nearer to Syene than those measurements place the military station Parembole. S. S.

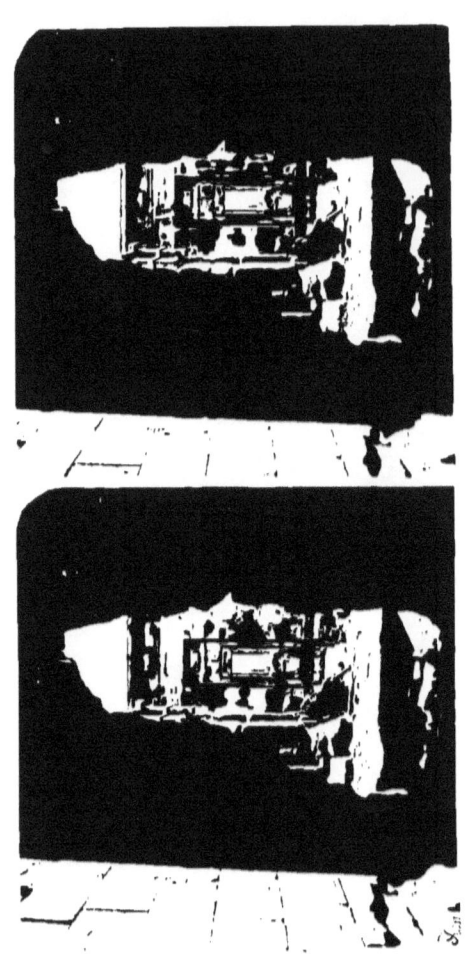

PLATE LXIV.

Interior of the Temple of Dabod.

THIS is a view from the interior of the central chamber, looking eastward. Here we have the three gates, and to the left the door-post into which was inserted the pivot of the bronze door of the portico. The square blocks in the curvetto mouldings over the gates would have been carved into the disks and serpents, if the work had not been arrested by the tottering condition of the Roman empire at the time of the construction. But a few years ago the roof of this chamber was perfect, as well as a great part of that of the portico; but whether its present condition is the effect of earthquake or wilful destruction it is impossible to say, our notices of this desolate country are so rare and imperfect.

J. B.

NOTE.—The unfinished state of the sculptures on this temple may be explained by the state of the country under the Romans. In the reign of Augustus the Ethiopians, under Queen Candace, who is mentioned in Acts, chap. viii., conquered Nubia and invaded Egypt. In the next reign, that of Tiberius, the Roman forces held quiet possession of these towns, and the hieroglyphical sculptures at Dabod were continued. But the attacks of the Ethiopians were soon afterwards repeated again and again, and trade sadly checked. In the time of Nero, the neighbouring parts of Ethiopia, beyond Nubia, were utterly ruined by the unceasing warfare of the barbarians. For a century longer the Romans kept their troops in Nubia, as a point of honour, rather than from any advantage arising from holding it.

LXIV.—INTERIOR OF THE TEMPLE OF DABOD.

But in the reign of Diocletian they finally gave it up, and from that time Syene was the southerly limit of the empire. From this account we can understand why few or no hieroglyphics were sculptured at Dabod after the reign of Tiberius.

S. S.

PLATE LXV.

The Temple of Kardassy — Nubia.

DISTANT view of the temple of Kardassy, looking northward. This is one of the most elegant ruins in the world, both on account of the variety of the capitals of its columns and its situation on an elevated rocky promontory, overlooking the river. There is a remarkable long slender roof-stone reaching from the architrave of one side of the temple to that of the other, a length of stone for which there would have been no necessity if it had been intended to build a chamber within the columns, for in that case the roof-stones would have rested on the walls of this cella or chamber. The circumstance of this remarkable long block of stone makes it almost probable that this temple, and that called the Bed of Pharaoh, which is not above twenty feet wide, was nothing more than a kind of inclosed square portico, or stone umbrella, admirably adapted to a country which, during the hottest hours of the day, was for so great a part of the year under an almost vertical sun. In this case, and in that of Philæ, they were on the coast and in the vicinity of other buildings, to which they might have been connected as landing-places or oratories for the sailors.

The columns that sustain the door-posts have a capital composed of the head of Athor or Isis, surmounted by a temple, the entrance to which is guarded by a serpent. The example we have chosen is taken from a temple at Philæ, in which the head of Athor is placed on a capital imitating the lotus flower; and so far it differs from the columns of Dendera and Kardassy. (See fig. 54.) Those at the sides are of a variety of the composite order, and were five in number, counting the angle columns; and these are joined by the intercolumnar walls. There are no hieroglyphics on the walls to tell us to whom it was intended to

LXV.—THE TEMPLE OF KARDASSY—NUBIA.

dedicate the temple; but judging from the columns of the door jambs, it would have been Athor or Isis, favourite divinities in Nubia of the

Fig. 54.

Ptolemaic and Roman periods. The distant mountains of the eastern desert, which are of a fine sandstone, and the trees on this and the opposite bank, are most delicately expressed. The beautiful sandstone formation is conspicuous in two inclined surfaces, where there are none of those small fragments with which the more horizontal surfaces are covered.

J. B.

NOTE.—Our account of the ruined state of Nubia, which explains the absence of sculpture from Dabod, explains also its absence from Kardassy. It is only wonderful that the inhabitants should have ever begun such a beautiful building, under circumstances so discouraging as those which surrounded them under the later Ptolemies and Roman emperors.

S. S.

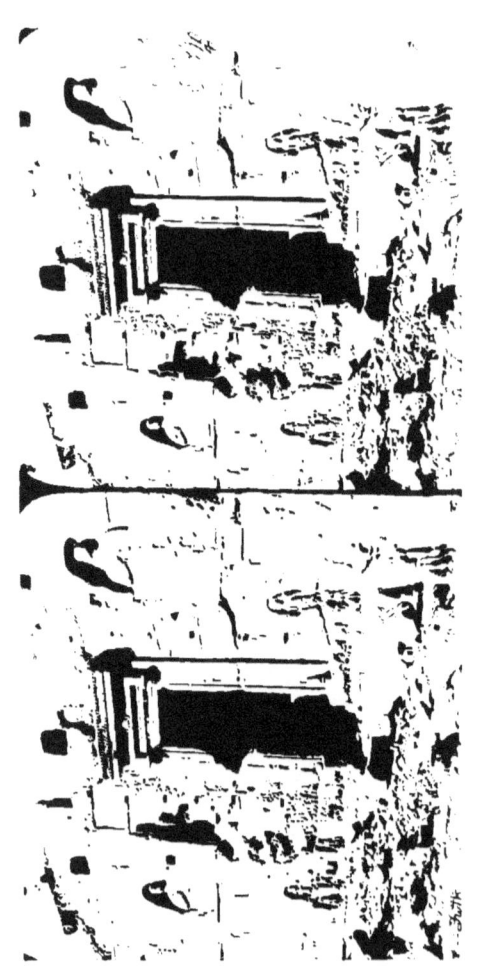

PLATE LXVI.

Tablets in the Quarries at Kardassy.

VIEW of a very interesting part of the sandstone quarries of Kardassy where there is a little oratory for the workmen cut in the rock during the Roman period, as may be presumed from the style of the mouldings surrounding the opening. The three large holes above the oratory were for the insertion of the stems of date-trees, which were supported at the other end by other timbers or stone piers—gerite or date branches being laid across them, and then mats, and clay, and stones, so as to make a permanent awning for those who came to worship. The smaller holes were for the scaffolding for those who engraved the inscriptions. The inscriptions are in the Greek language, inclosed in a Roman-formed tablet. The busts in the two niches are probably those of Roman consuls who were benefactors to the province and workmen. The figures carved out of rock near the ground are the boyish attempts of the workmen to imitate the Egyptian sculpture. Probably Greek and Roman malefactors were among the workmen, and in consequence we have the Greek writing and Roman architecture. The road from the quarry to the Nile is a regular incline ; and much of the stone used in the buildings of Philæ came from this place, it being easier to float down the river on rafts than to bring it from Silsilis in ships.

J. B.

LXVI.—TABLETS IN THE QUARRIES AT KARDASSY.

NOTE.—The sandstone quarries of Kardassy were actively worked during the first two centuries and a half of the Christian era; and it was probably for the sake of these quarries that the Romans chiefly thought any part of Nubia worth holding. The inscriptions, which are all in the Greek language, are usually ungrammatical; and, if we may judge from the names of the pious writers, they were the works of native Egyptians. In every case they are by the head of the workmen, who styles himself priest or chief-priest of the freight, meaning the stone which was being shipped off from the quarries. He seems to have held this office of a priest usually for a year, though sometimes for several years; and as it was an office of honour, accompanied with some expense: he adds with pride in his inscription how much he spent in supporting it. One of these boastful inscriptions tells us that Macrinus, in the eight years that he took upon himself this expensive office, spent two hundred and forty pieces of gold, and adds that no one ever has or ever will spend so much.

S. S.

PLATE LXVII.

The Temple of Kalabshe.

TEMPLE of Kalabshe, looking southwards. This is a charmingly selected view of one of the most entire ruins of Nubia.

It gives a very good idea of the closed-up box-like exterior of an Egyptian temple (see fig. 55), besides exhibiting a gradation of tint that no painter could desire to mend. The view is taken from an eminence near the path leading up to a small ancient temple,

Fig. 55.

called Beyt el Wali, partly excavation and partly construction, executed in the time of Rameses II. It was probably built on his return from the conquest of some warlike tribes in the interior of Africa, who wore leopard skins and used long-bows.

The conquered people of those southern provinces of the Egyptian empire are described by Herodotus exactly as we find them represented on the walls of this ancient temple. In the mummy-room of the British Museum we have casts from these very interesting historical sculptures, which were presented by Mr. Robert Hay, of Linplum. This large temple of Kalabshe, of which the view is before us, is of massive construction, and surrounded by a double wall of great thickness and of admirable masonry, of the time of the Roman dominion. It is not improbable that it served as a fortress as well as a sacred edifice.

It consists of a beautifully proportioned portico of six columns of the composite order, three deep; behind the portico a large chamber, with four columns; and behind this several dark chambers. In front of the portico

LXVII.—THE TEMPLE OF KALABSHE.

is a large court, surrounded by columns, and joined to the pyramidal towers of the principal entrance by a high wall, in which are small dark chambers. This high wall, proceeding from the back of the pyramidal towers, surrounds the sacred edifice, leaving a considerable space between it and the block containing the rooms at the back of the portico; and a door on this side of the court may be seen in this view, leading into the area of the second inclosure, the wall of which has been thrown down. The plan of this temple so much resembles that of all the Ptolemaic and Roman temples generally, that we have supplied that of Edfu (see fig. 56) to make the description more intelligible. This outer wall, which is a considerable distance from that next the temple, is joined to the two ends of the pyramidal towers; and it has two gates in front and one in each side, opposite to the lateral entrance into the first court. Descending to the river the whole width of the front is a wide terrace, paved, and built of massive stones.

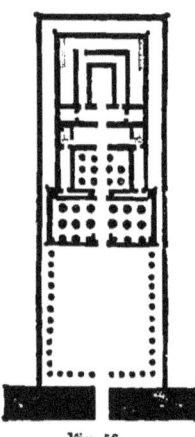

Fig. 56.

From the roof of the lower part of the temple is a flight of steps leading up to the roof of the portico, on which are the remains of brick constructions, the dwellings of the chiefs, religious or secular, of the Christian population that occupied this stronghold at the time of the Arabian conquest. A little south of the temple may be seen a perpendicular excavation in the rock, which is the quarry out of which the stones were taken for the temple; and near the group of Arabs, to the north may be seen the remains of another quarry, now filled up with the chippings and fragments of blocks of other constructions; and between it and the temple the walls of the houses of the present inhabitants. From the north end of the terrace there proceeds into the Nile a thick wall of massive unhewn blocks of stone, several yards long, which can only be seen at low Nile. A similar wall occurs on this side of the river in Nubia, at a few miles apart, as marked in the valuable map of the country published some years ago by Messrs. Parke and Scoles.

LXVII.—THE TEMPLE OF KALABSHE.

North of Kalabshe the river is bounded by rocks called Bab el Kalabshe, which, during the low Nile, produce a rapidity of current sometimes difficult to pass. In front is a group of two date-trees and a doum-tree, which is a kind of palm producing a fruit in shape and size like a potato, having an edible crust that tastes like gingerbread.

The two projections at the back of the lower temple and at the sides would have been carved into lions with extended fore-paws, and a channel to relieve the roof of the water produced by the occasional and rare showers. The same provision is made in the walls of the temple of Karnak and Dendera.

It should also be mentioned that there are indications of a more ancient structure having existed on this site, in the time of the Pharaohs. All the architrave stones, and many others used in the walls of this temple, are joined together with large wooden cramps made of the wood of the gum-arabic tree, which is excessively hard and heavy. These cramps are inserted into a cavity of the shape of the cramp itself, half in one stone and half in the other: the cramp being wider at each end, the stones cannot be separated. In the collection of the Royal Institute of British Architects is one of these cramps perfectly sound, taken out of a wall built in the time of the third Rameses at Medinet-Habon, which cannot be less than 1050 years before our era, and consequently now 2911 years old.

J. B.

PLATE LXVIII.

Interior of the Temple of Kalabshe.

View of the interior of the temple of Kalabshe. A great deal of the sculpture, like all the temples of Nubia, is unfinished. At this period also a low-rilievo seems to have been preferred to the more ancient Egyptian style of sculpture peculiar to Egypt.

There is a want of vigour in the forms, a thickness in the proportions, that distinguishes all the sculpture of this period from that of the Pharaonic times, that is conspicuous in that of this building.

J. B.

Note.—Kalabshe is the ancient Talmis, thirty-five miles from Syene. The sculptures on the temple are of the time of the emperors, from Augustus to Severus. They are very much in relief, not in sunk relief like the usual Egyptian sculptures. The Greek inscriptions are by the Roman soldiers, who were quartered there in the time of the early emperors; they are addressed to the great god Mandouli, on behalf of the writer, his family, his friends, and sometimes his horse, and sometimes the reader. Mandouli was probably the god Mando-ra of the Egyptians.

A more important Greek inscription here is by Silco, king of the Nubians, in the fifth century, who boasts of his victories over the more barbarous and more idolatrous Blemmyes. From this we learn how entirely civilization was driven out of that now ruined country.

S. S.

PLATE LXIX.

Temple of Kalabshe—Second Entrance.

INTERIOR of Kalabshe, second view. The style of architecture in this doorway is nearly the same as the last, but with the addition of a moulding below the figure of the winged sun. The sculpture, which is in relief, represents the emperor presenting his offerings to the gods of the country; but it was so far left unfinished, that it does not tell us the names of the gods. In front of each god, near to his head, may be seen a rectangular tablet, sometimes wide enough for two vertical lines of hieroglyphics, and sometimes for only one line, which would if cut give us the god's name and titles. The god Chem, the Priapus of the Romans, may be recognized by his left arm raised high above his head; and over that hand is a whip, which, however, he does not hold. This god is the peculiar god of the country, and he takes his name from Chemi, *Egypt*, which, indeed, is the same name as that of Ham, the son of Noah, from whom, the Book of Genesis tells us, the Egyptians were descended.

The very fracture of the stones is here shown most satisfactorily. The geologist may almost study the nature of the sandstone of which the temple was built. It is the sandstone rock of the whole district, through which the granite has burst forth on both sides, at the north forming the cataract of Syene, and at the south the cataract of Abousimbel.

S. S.

PLATE LXX.

The Temple of Dandour.

VIEW of the north-east corner of the portico in front of the temple of Dandour. This temple, which is only a few miles south of Kalabshe, and on the western bank of the river, is entirely of Roman times. The portico consists of two columns within the side walls of the cubiform building. To this succeeds three small chambers, and another excavated out of the rock. An opening has been made through the wall of the temple into the side of the portico, where the sculpture ceased to be regarded as sacred or historical. The wall is divided into two compartments from the cornice to the dado. In the upper, the emperor is repeated, making offerings to two divinities, who are in a sitting position. In the lower compartment two divinities like the emperor himself are standing. The dado is composed of the papyrus in various stages of growth, and at regular intervals a figure of Nilus: showing the great esteem and importance in which that production of the Nile was held in the Roman times. On the pavement at this corner are lines made to certify the place of the corner-stone, and the rectangular position of the walls. High up is a mark of the plaster cast of the head of the emperor Trajan, which was taken thirty years ago, still unobliterated. The sun shines on this wall, and on that of the other side of the temple at one and the same time for several days in the year, this place being just under the tropic of Capricorn. The pylon in front was joined to a wall which surrounded the temple, of which we see the wanton destruction in the vast amount of fragments that encumber this ruin; and still farther are the massive blocks of the admirably constructed terrace which reaches to the river. The front wall of this terrace presents a concave and inclined surface to the river, like that already described in front of the bed of Pharaoh, and is of admirable construction.

J. B.

PLATE LXXI.

The Temple of Gerf.

VIEW of a row of Osiride figures which supported the roof of a portico which led up to the excavated chambers of the temple of Gerf Husseyn. These figures, and others similar, formed the sides of a court joining the towers of the gateway in front of a large excavated temple of Rameses mai Amun. From the pylon in front, there must have been a long flight of steps to the town below. This ruin, like the last, is on the western bank of the Nile, and consequently the opposite mountains are those of the eastern Desert. The ceiling of the large chamber of this temple is supported by two rows of colossal figures of this Pharaoh of the short heavy Nubian proportions of these built figures in the portico. To this chamber succeeds a second, whose ceiling is supported by two piers; this chamber gives access to two side chambers and a small one in the centre, against the back of which are sitting figures of the gods of the temple, and the king, which are Pthah and Pasht, and another goddess.

J. B.

NOTE.—Gerf Husseyn is the ancient Tutzis. The temple was built by Rameses II., whose name may be seen in our photograph. The Ptolemies seem to have made no addition to it; and it was wholly neglected by the Romans, who had no troops stationed so far south.

S. S.

PLATE LXXII.

The Temple of Dakkeh.

DAKKEH is a remarkably elegant ruin, before which stands a gate, with its almost perfect pyramidal towers. It is built on the western bank of the Nile, about ten miles from Gerf Husseyn. In the view before us the distinguishing features of the earlier and later styles of sculpture are well shown. Those on the wall to the left, at right angles to the wall on the right, are of the late Roman style, giving a puffy, rounded contour to the figure, while the sculpture on the right has a firmer, less puffy contour, yet by no means possessing the vigour of the style of the time of the Pharaohs. The base of the wall is ornamented with figures of Nilus, carrying two water-vessels, between bouquets of lotus-flowers. This building, like all the ancient temples of Nubia, bears unequivocal indications of its conversion to a Christian place of worship. On the wall of the portico are the pictures of several saints, amongst which a well-preserved representation of St. George and the Dragon. Two small doors have been cut through the intercolumnar walls of this portico, by way of accommodating it to the new worship.

J. B.

NOTE.—Dakkeh is the Pselcis of the Greeks; it is ten miles from Tutzis. This place fell under the Ptolemies in the reign of the third king of that name, Ptolemy Euergetes. Since the fall of the family of Rameses, Ethiopia and Nubia had been independent of Egypt. Psammetichus I. or II. had attempted an invasion; Cambyses had attempted an invasion. The people of those regions had paid a small nominal tribute to Darius;

LXXII.—THE TEMPLE AT DAKKEH.

but they had been separated from Egypt for many centuries. The walls of the temples of Nubia declare the history of the place. Rameses II. had carved his name and titles at Tutzis; and Ptolemy Euergetes, nine centuries afterwards, was the next king of Egypt who did the same, at this temple of Pselcis, within a distance of ten miles.

Pselcis continued an important place under the early Roman emperors; and among the ruins near the temple have been discovered a number of tiles, on each of which is written, in Greek, the receipt or discharge for the allowance of wine, corn, and money, which the general had as his monthly pay.

The later inscriptions are dedications to the god Hermes, who is explained to be Taut-n-p-Nubs, or Thoth of Nubia.

The king upon his knees, in our photograph, presenting an offering to the god, is one of the Roman emperors, most probably Augustus; but the characters within the oval, where we hope to find his name, contain only a title. The temple was built under the Ptolemies, in honour of the god Thoth, or Hermes. The place was soon deserted by the Romans, as too far south for them to hold; and the Greek inscriptions found there are not so much of residents, as of travellers who came so far to look at the buildings, in the second century of our era.

Here we are still within the Dodecaschœnos, the district over which the early Roman emperors claimed control. Our next photograph will take us beyond that district.

S. S.

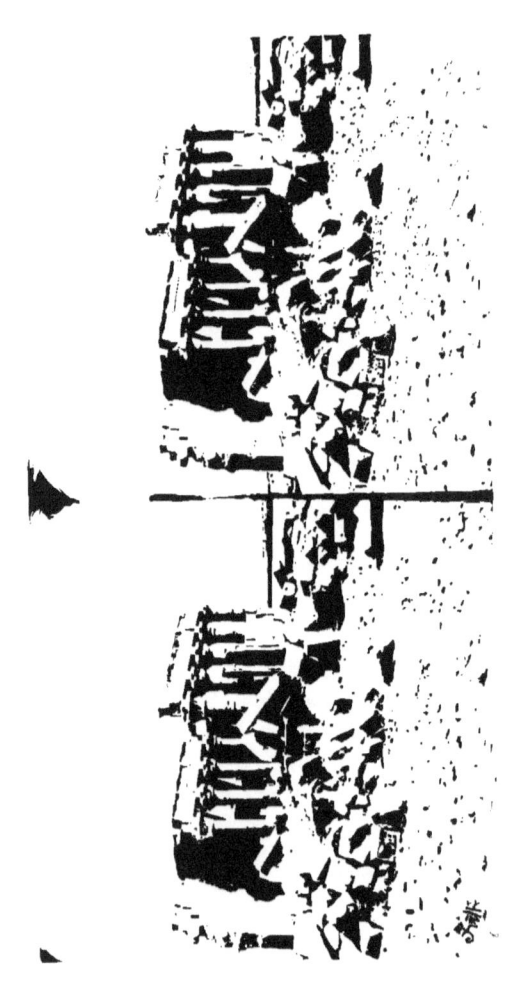

PLATE LXXIII.

The Temple of Maharraka — General View.

THIS ruin is a few miles south of Dakkeh, and on the same side of the river. It consists of two rows of columns, and one wall,—the end walls and columns having only recently fallen; but the wall which stood behind the columns on the right hand had many years ago been thrown down, apparently by an earthquake, every stone lying in its position on the ground. No part of this hypæthral building was ever finished, the capitals only blocked out. From an examination of the ruins, it appears that it consisted of six columns at the sides, and four at the ends.

Near to this ruin, but more to the right, were other ruins; and on a wall of good masonry, to the right, was engraved a group of Isis and Horus, sitting under the sacred fig-tree,—resembling the early pictures of the Madonna and Child, there being a degree of perspective attained in the drawing of the figure which was never sought or attained by the more ancient Egyptian artists.

J. B.

NOTE.—Maharraka is the Hierasycaminon of the Greeks, so named from the sacred tree of the place. The Greek inscriptions are to Isis with ten thousand names, and the sun, Serapis, written by soldiers stationed there in the time of the Antonines.

This is the most southerly place on the banks of the Nile in which we find any Greek inscriptions cut by either Greek or Roman soldiers stationed there. Neither Ptolemy nor Emperor attempted to hold the country beyond Hierasycaminon.

LXXIII.—THE TEMPLE OF MAHARRAKA—GENERAL VIEW.

Hierasycaminon is seventy miles, or twelve schœni, beyond Syene; and hence this portion of Nubia, which the Romans thought it worth while to hold, was called the Dodecaschœnos. They held it till the reign of Commodus. After that time its fate is unknown, till, in the reign of Diocletian, one hundred years later, it is formally given up to the Nubians, by the withdrawal of the Roman troops to Elephantine.

S. S.

PLATE LXXIV.

The Temple of Maharraka — Side View.

ANOTHER view of the same ruin, looking more directly eastward across the Nile. Both these pictures serve to illustrate the construction, which is here shown in a woodcut (see fig. 57). Half the architrave stone is occupied by the cornice stone, the other by the roof stones, the other end of which rest on the wall. The corner column had to support the ends of three architrave stones, as may be easily conceived, and it would thereby be a weak point in the construction, which was sometimes obviated by placing an extra column, as in an ancient example at Medinet-Habou.

Fig. 57.

J. B.

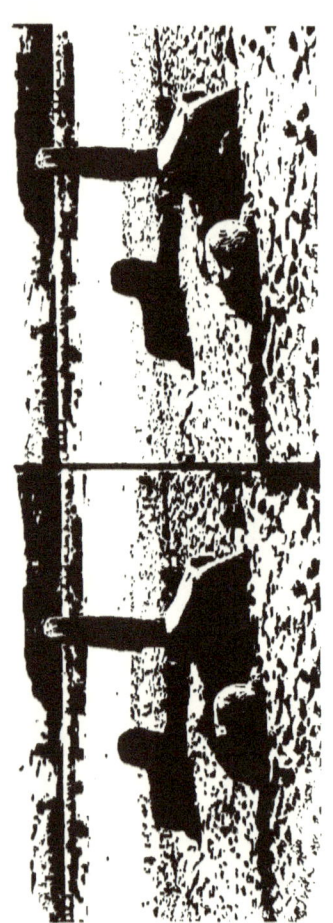

PLATE LXXV.

Wady Sebouah, from the West.

WADY SEBOUAH, or the Valley of the Lion, so called by the natives on account of the avenue of lion sphinxes, which extends from the edge of the Desert to the front of the temple. Sebouah is a barren and sandy district, the mountains on both sides of the valley approaching the river, and on the west side, the sand much advanced beyond its ancient boundary, having buried the temple to a considerable height.

The ruins are very extensive, consisting in the first place of the avenue of sphinxes, of a propylon with its pyramidal towers entire, and of a large court behind, whose lateral porticos are supported by Osiride figures. To this succeed the several chambers, which had been converted into a Christian place of worship, since which time the sand of the Desert has so much increased as to have closed up the entrance. The larger chamber contained the figures of St. Peter and Paul, perfectly intact and fresh, as if painted only recently on the plaster by which the heathen sculpture had been covered.

In the view before us, we have the two last sphinxes on the right of the avenue terminated by a figure of Rameses, as we are informed by the legend engraved on the back of the figure, which can be distinctly read in the photograph.

J. B.

NOTE.—We are here beyond the Dodecaschœnos, or portion of the valley from Syeno to Hierasycaminon, measuring twelve schœni, or about

LXXV.—WADY SEBOUAH, FROM THE WEST.

seventy-two miles, which was the only portion of Nubia that the Roman emperors ever undertook to govern. On the fall of the Ptolemies, Sebouah, and all the towns to the south of it, were left to their own management, either to find a government for themselves, or to fall into a state of barbarism.

S. S.

PLATE LXXVI.

View at Wady Sebouah.

VIEW of the same, looking north across the avenue of sphinxes. Here we have the two figures of Rameses II., in the prescribed attitude of walking, the left leg advanced. No figure in the round has yet been discovered in a walking position, with the right leg before the left. The proportions of these figures are those generally observed by the Nubian sculptors of this age.

At the termination of the avenue, the direction of the wind is pointed out by the condition of the sand about the figures; so constant and accurate are the laws by which the phenomena of nature are governed.

J. B.

PLATE LXXVII.

The Temple of Wady Sebouah — General View.

A more general view of the Wady Sebouah, taken from the rocks at the back of the temple, the eye of the observer being on a level with the top of the pyramidal towers of the pylon. Nothing is to be desired respecting the distant mountains of the eastern Desert, or the gradation of tints: all that is wanted to complete the picture, and make this one of the most beautiful photographs in the collection, would be a group of Arabs in the foreground.

The Arabic language again appears in this district of Nubia, in all its purity; and its clear guttural masculine sounds strike the ear that has been used to the monotonous African dialects of Nubia, as peculiarly energetic.

J. B.

Note.—Our travellers have very naturally given their first attention to the great works of art in Egypt and Nubia, which were all made by Pagans; but it is to be wished that they would not wholly overlook those which were made by the Christians. The Christian works are all in a bad style of art, made by poor and oppressed people, and very little worth the artist's notice; but an account of them would contribute something to the history of civilization, or perhaps we must say to the history of the decline of civilization, in those parts. An examination of the Christian alterations made in this temple at Sebouah, might teach us when Christianity rose, and again when it fell in this part of Nubia, beyond the dominion of the Romans.

S. S.

PLATE LXXVIII.

The small Rock Temple at Abou Simbel.

ENTRANCE to the smaller temple of Abou Simbel. This temple, like the last, is situated on the western bank of the Nile, and about seventy-five miles south of it. It is wholly hollowed out of the rock. On each side of the door are three niches, containing two erect colossal statues of Rameses II., accompanied by his sons, and one erect colossal statue of the queen, accompanied by her daughters. The king wears the crowns of Upper and Lower Egypt on the north side of the door, and that of Upper Egypt alone on the south side of the door. In the two end niches he wears the cap of Osiris. Both the statues of the queen wear the head-dress of the goddess Athor. All these statues are cut out of the face of the rock, and are very superior in their proportions to the generality of those executed in Nubia. The entrance is not adorned with the usual curvetto moulding, but immediately over the lintel is a row of guardian serpents. The lintel is adorned with a representation of the king, offering to Athor on the right, and Amun on the left. The door-jambs are decorated with a single line of hieroglyphics, in which the prænomen of Rameses II. is conspicuous. There is also an inscription on the surface of the rock, between each figure and above the niches. The entire depth of the excavation is about ninety feet. The roof of the first chamber is supported by six piers, adorned with the head of Athor; behind this a chamber, giving access to one central and two lateral chapels; the central having the fore-part of a cow projecting from the wall, as we see Athor represented in the Papyri and funeral tablets, as if coming out of the mountains of the western side of the Nile. The sculptures on the walls are all religious, and of the most elegant type.

J. B.

PLATE LXXIX.

Colossal Figure of the Queen at the small Temple at Abou Simbel.

THE figure of the queen of Rameses II. and her two daughters. Notwithstanding the necessity of turning up the camera to obtain this view, there being so little space between the figure and the precipitous rock, at whose base flows the river, we have the elegant and vigorous forms of the figure belonging to this age well delineated. The lower part of the figure is of course larger than it would be if it had not been necessary to turn up the camera, and make the horizon in the sky.

J. B.

NOTE.—To this colossal figure of the Egyptian queen has been given the head of a cow, in order to represent her in the character of the goddess Athor. She wears the tight, transparent dress of the Egyptian ladies. The line of hieroglyphics, at her right-hand side, is the same as that on the left-hand side of the king in the last picture. The two pictures there join one another.

We now find no rock-hewn temples in Egypt, but we must suppose that the cave was the original form of the temple there, because it was to Egypt that both Ethiopia and Sinai were indebted for their art; and placed as Egypt is, between the rock-hewn temples of Abou Simbel in Nubia, and Sarabet el Cadem in Sinai, we cannot but believe that the models for both those temples were to be found there. Indeed, the cave tombs of Benihassan may, very likely, have been made originally for temples. Other cave temples may have been destroyed by the more vigorous working of the

LXXIX.—COLOSSAL FIGURE OF THE QUEEN AT ABOU SIMBEL.

stone quarries, because every rock-hewn temple was assuredly made exactly in that spot where it was convenient to cut out more stone; and, as the progress of civilization is always the chief cause of the destruction of antiquities, so probably the opening the vast quarries for building the great temples of Upper Egypt may have destroyed any cave temples before hollowed out of the hill. The first opening of a quarry would form a cave temple, and the farther working of the quarry would destroy it.

S. S.

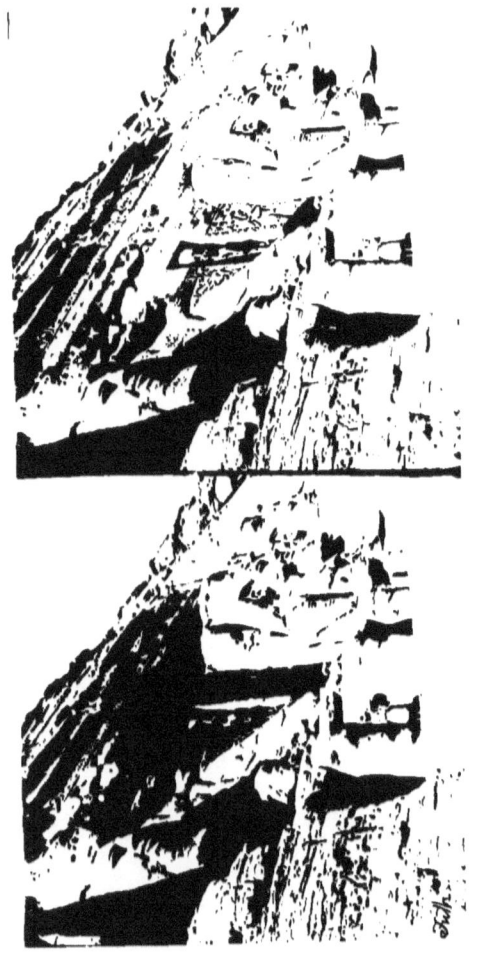

PLATE LXXX.

The Great Rock Temple of Abou Simbel.

THIS extraordinary work of engineering and the sculptor's art is situated on the west bank of the Nile, next door to the last described temple, and about 650 miles from the coast of the Mediterranean. It was first discovered by Burckhardt, about forty years ago, on his return from Berber. At that time all the figures were buried in the moving sand of the Libyan desert to their chins; and as he was travelling in the guise of a Mahommedan, any very particular examination of the place would have subjected him to the suspicion of being a Frank. On his arrival in Cairo, he informed Mr. Salt, the British Consul, of his discovery; and a plan was devised for sending Mr. Belzoni, who was acquainted with the language and prejudices of the people, to make researches on the spot. After a second journey and many delays and difficulties, Mr. Belzoni succeeded in removing the sand sufficiently to creep in at the top of the door; and great was his surprise to find a large chamber, 55 feet long by 48 wide, the ceiling of which was supported by eight colossal figures, the walls covered with religious and historical pictures, all the colours in perfect preservation. To this chamber succeeded another, 37 feet wide by 24 feet deep, whose ceiling was supported by four piers; and to this succeeded another of the same width, but only 9 feet deep, which gave entrance to three small chambers, the centre one about 12 feet wide by about 20 feet deep. In the middle of this chamber was an altar standing in front of four sitting statues; viz. Pthah, Amun-ra, the King, and Horus.

The other two chambers were less in size, but in the one to the right was a much defaced, unfinished sitting statue. Four small doors in the great chamber led to eight narrow chambers with a high ledge or table and square niches. The first Europeans, who went into this underground temple, the discovery and description of which appeared to them more like one of the

LXXX.—THE GREAT ROCK TEMPLE OF ABOU SIMBEL.

stories in the Arabian Nights than a reality, were Belzoni, Lord and Lady Belmore, and Capt. Beechey. Subsequently Mr. Robert Hay, of Linplum, uncovered the two southernmost statues to their bases, measured and drew the whole temple, and made a cast of the northernmost head, which is still white with the stain of the plaster, although done more than thirty years ago. About the year 1836, this cast and several others, now in the mummy room, were presented by that gentleman to the nation. A model, full size, of two of these figures, has since been made in the Crystal Palace.

The whole height of the façade is about 95 and its width 110 feet.

Above the curvetto is a row of monkeys more than six feet high, in the attitude of adoring the sun. Below the curvetto and torus is the dedication, by Rameses II., of the temple to Amun-ra, and the other gods of the temple, in large incavo hieroglyphics. The four colossal figures of Rameses II. are sitting at the gate or entrance, the place where, it will be seen by reference to the plan of temples already passed, the statues of the kings are always placed, in obedience to an ancient custom, from which the metaphor in Genesis xxii. 17 is derived.

These colossi, as we shall see, have three other statues attached to them, like those in the plain of Thebes and the colossus of the Memnonium, the mother and wife at the side of the throne, the son between the feet of the father: this also embodying an ancient custom, from which the metaphor, used in the same book (xlix. 10), denoting succession or descent, is derived. Again, to complete this metaphorical sculpture, the block on which these colossi place their feet is adorned with the figures of the different peoples or races, enemies of Egypt; likewise, in obedience to an ancient custom from which is derived the metaphor so often used in the sacred writings to denote conquest and entire subjection.

J. B.

NOTE.—The valley of the Nile in Nubia is so narrow, and the strip of land which can be cultivated so small, that a very scanty population is all that could ever have lived there, without the help of foreign trade and home

LXXX.—THE GREAT ROCK TEMPLE OF ABOU SIMBEL.

manufactures. And both of these advantages were possessed by Nubia in the time of the great kings of the name of Amunothph, Thothmosis, and Rameses. While the Nubian gold mines were worked successfully by these kings of Egypt, these Nubian towns enjoyed the advantages of a highly paid carrying trade; and labour was attracted to Abou Simbel more particularly, to forward the boats or their burdens over the second cataract, which is a few miles higher up the river. The home manufacture of Abou Simbel and the other towns of Nubia was in their sandstone quarries; and while Syene, Philœ, and Elephantine were populous and wealthy, the quarry-men of Nubia enjoyed a prosperous trade. Nor were the workmen in the quarry a very low and unskilled class. They included the sculptors who made the statues and carved the small tablets, and the scribes who drew the hieroglyphics for the sculptors to cut. There can be no doubt that these large temples which we have been admiring, hollowed out of the rock at Abou Simbel, were the quarries out of which the building stone was cut for the neighbourhood of Philœ, and for many statues and tablets for sale in Egypt. Such skilled workmen would naturally show their skill in their own town, and as they were officers of the crown, they made these colossal statues of the king at the entrance, and made the pillars, which support the roof, in the form of statues of the same king. The priests of the freight or of the quarry, whom we have spoken of when describing Kardassy—for such was the rank of the chief of the workmen, and such the sacerdotal form of government—made the quarry into a temple dedicated to the great god Amun-ra. And in this way only we are able to explain how these large and highly ornamented and costly temples are to be seen in a spot which now will hardly maintain the poverty of a handful of scattered villagers.

S. S.

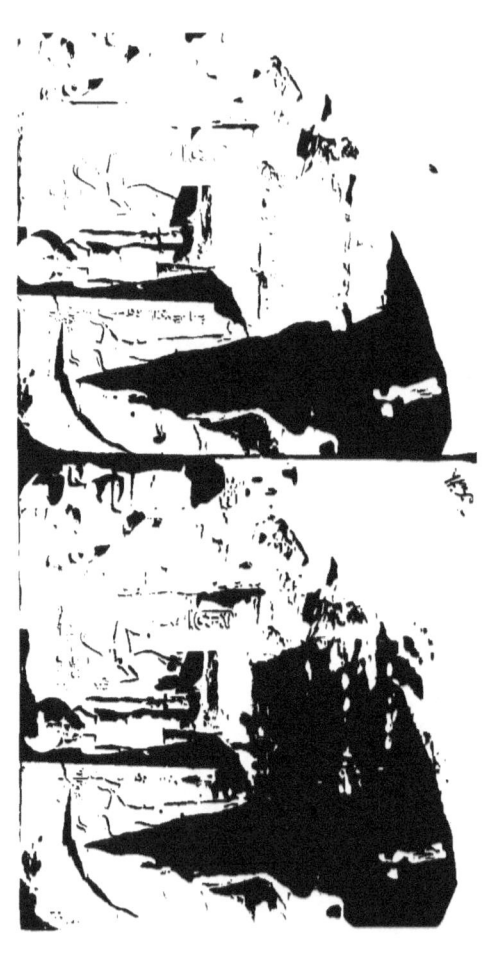

PLATE LXXXI.

Entrance to the Great Rock Temple at Abou Simbel.

NEARER view of the two central colossi, or those next the entrance. The colossus to the left fell in consequence of some movement in the substratum of the mountain out of which it is sculptured, whether by earthquake or other geological phenomenon of ancient date, before the Parthenon of Phidias was built. Satisfactory evidence of this statement is to be gathered from the present condition of the temple, which we shall endeavour to describe, with other curious particulars, in the course of examining the beautiful series before us.

The countenance of the colossus to the right is second in beauty of expression to the southernmost. They all look down, with a majestic calmness, on the mighty stream that flows at their feet; but there is a benignity of expression, particularly in the profile view of the southern countenance, that excels all other Egyptian works, and is scarcely surpassed in Grecian art. In this photograph the figure of the hawk-headed divinity Ra, with the disk of the sun on his head, is of excellent sculpture. On his right is the fox-headed staff, and under his left hand was the figure of Temai, the goddess of Truth and Justice. Towards the square niche containing these elements of the royal name the king (on both sides, for the sake of uniformity,) offers a little image of the goddess of Truth. It is curious to observe the *pentimento*, as the Italians call that artistic change of mind which a second line discloses. The upper groove or outline of the king's head-dress was the line adopted by the ancient sculptor who had filled up the lower one with plaster, now fallen out, disclosing his change of mind. Nor should it be forgotten to remark the royal title, so legible on the shoulder of the colossus, because it is always on the shoulders of Egyptian statues of kings that the name and title are engraved, the shoulder being the

LXXXI.—ENTRANCE TO THE GREAT ROCK TEMPLE AT ABOU SIMBEL.

place on which a man carries the greatest weight with most security and ease ; and hence the place on which the king wears the badge of honour, the sign of authority and government, and from which the metaphor, in reference to the Messiah, in Isaiah, ix. 6, is derived. The figure of the Arab sitting on the sand that covers the lap of the colossus affords some idea of its dimensions. Lower down is the top of the entrance, and nearer is another figure of a Nubian leaning against the colossus, on the left hand of the entrance, on whose leg is engraved the most ancient piece of Greek writing known, recording the visit of certain Greek soldiers in the pay of Psammetichus, who had been sent in pursuit of the rebellious troops of the garrison of Elephantine. The revolt of the garrison is mentioned by Herodotus, and thus this curious inscription confirms his account of the rebellion and flight of the garrison; and at the same time goes far to corroborate the statement already made, that the upper part of this statue had already fallen before the inscription was engraved, because it is written obliquely over the calf of the leg, showing that the sand had already covered the fallen fragments of the colossus, B.C. 650, about which time it was engraved; that is, about 150 years before the Parthenon of Phidias was built. Other curious circumstantial evidences will be pointed out as they appear.   J. B.

NOTE.—The Greek inscription on the shin of the great statue is as follows :—

"When King Psammetichus came to Elephantine, those who were with Psammetichus, the son of Theocles, wrote this. They sailed and they came beyond Kerkis where the river ceases ; namely, a foreigner named Dechepotasimpto, and an Egyptian named Amasis. Damearchon, the son of Amoibichus, and Pelephus, the son of Oulamus, wrote it."

If this march into Nubia took place in the reign of Psammetichus I. in the year B.C. 658-614, it is one of the earliest Greek inscriptions known.

S. S.

PLATE LXXXII.

Colossal Statue of Rameses, Abou Simbel.

VIEW of the most southern of the colossi of Abou Simbel. Part of the dedication, in large hieroglyphics, in which the name of Rameses occurs, is perfectly distinct. Admirably defined is the little figure of the Nubian sailor, whom prudence forbids to advance farther on the dangerous surface of the colossal knee, to exhibit the contrast it forms with his own. The head of the statue of the son of Rameses II. just appears between the legs of the colossus, and the upper part of the statue of his mother. Still more to the left of this picture, is the moulding on the top of a tablet.

J. B.

NOTE.—These colossal statues are not altogether made according to the same proportions as the statues of Egypt. The Theban artists, and those who worked in the quarries of Syene, divided the sitting statue into fifteen parts. Of these they gave to the height of the seat, or under part of the thigh, five measures from the ground. The point of the knee was at the sixth measure; the top of the hip at the seventh; the bottom of the neck at the twelfth; and the top of the head at the fifteenth. But the Nubian artist has made his figure stouter and more clumsy. Thus if we give, as before, five measures to the seat, or under part of the thigh, we find the whole is only fourteen measures and a half high. And instead of three measures being given to the head and neck, the chin is brought down to the shoulder, and three measures are given to the head

LXXXII.—COLOSSAL STATUE OF RAMESES AT ABOU SIMBEL.

alone. It follows the same faulty rule of making the length, from the back of the body to the front of the knee, equal to the length from the ground to the top of the knee; thus making the thigh too short. We find the same clumsy proportions given to most of the statues in Ethiopia.

S. S.

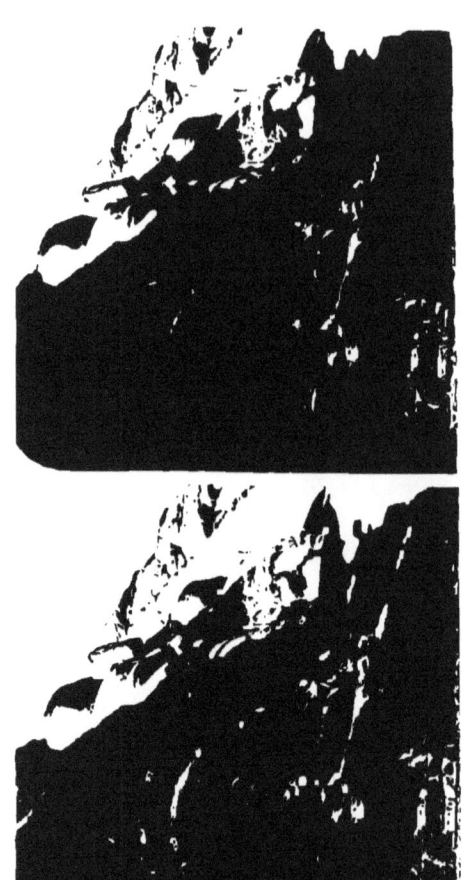

PLATE LXXXIII.

Western Figure on the Great Rock Temple at Abou Simbel.

VIEW of the colossus on the right of the entrance, and the head of the most northern, of which we have a cast on the staircase of the British Museum. A fissure, going obliquely from the back of the shoulder to midway between the elbow and wrist of the right arm of this statue, we are certain took place before the end of the reign of the successor of the great Rameses, for the blocks of stone built up from the seat to the elbow, to support the threatened limb, bear the name Rameses III. The dip or inclination of this fissure is the same as that of the fractured surface of the fallen colossus, and likewise the same as a fissure which crosses the farthest colossal statue, on the left side of the great hall, between which and its companion, to save it, has been built a wall, adorned with a tablet, bearing the date of the king, whose name appears in the hieroglyphics; so that certain it is, ruin threatened the celebrated shrine at that time; if, indeed, the avalanche of the colossus on the left of the entrance was not the consequence of the same geological phenomenon which produced the rent. We will terminate this already long account, by a few words on the historical pictures on the walls of the great hall. The whole of the wall to the right is occupied by an incised picture, representing the same battle and camp scene as that engraved on the outside of the towers of the gate of Luxor (see Plate 28), and on the inside of the towers of the gate of the Memnonium, as likewise on the wall of the portico of the second court of the last-named edifice.

This picture is published in the great work of Rosellini, as well as all the other historical pictures of this chamber, and to that work we shall

LXXXIII.—WESTERN FIGURE ON THE GREAT ROCK TEMPLE.

refer our readers who desire to examine the interesting matter in question to which we are about to allude. The left-hand wall is divided into an upper and lower compartment: the upper, set apart for religious subjects; the lower, occupied by several pictures representing the king going out to war, attended by his body-guard and a lion, as recorded by Herodotus. Then the attack and subjugation of a light-complexioned race, inhabiting a mountainous country; then the picture to which we are about to refer,

Fig. 58.

and, lastly, the return of the king to Egypt, bringing with him groups of prisoners, highly interesting in an ethnological point of view, as specimens of the various nations and peoples which he had subjugated belonging to Asia and Africa, and possibly also to the continent of Europe, brought to grace his triumph. All these various nations again appear in two allegorical pictures, one on each side the entrance, representing the king about

LXXXIII.—WESTERN FIGURE ON THE GREAT ROCK TEMPLE.

to cut off the heads of all his enemies, in the presence of the great divinity of Egypt, who stretches forth his hand in aid. The place of this allegorical picture is always the gate; and the whole design is, as it were, an embodiment of the highly figurative language of the Psalms, particularly Psalm xviii. 40. (See Fig. 58.)

The picture to which we now beg your attention is represented by the little wood-cut in the margin. This spirited composition, of which the figures are as large as life, and a few years ago perfect in colour and details, is among the others, no less perfect, on the left-hand wall of the great chamber of this extraordinary excavation. The same composition, somewhat smaller, is sculptured, in bold Egyptian incavo rilievo, on the north wall of the temple of Karnak; and there this deed of valour is attributed to Oimenepthah I., whose tomb was discovered by Belzoni, and whose sarcophagus is in the Soane Museum. Here, however, it is attributed to his son, Rameses II. The people with whom the king is contending are of gigantic stature, as we gather from representations of them in other places, and because in no other instance are the enemies of the king so nearly equal to himself in dimensions. They are of light complexion, blue eyes, and wearing a remarkable lock of hair, fashioned beard, and tatooed skin. We learn from Leviticus xix. 27, and xxi. 5, that the Israelites were forbidden to adopt certain fashions, common to the people among whom they were to come into contact on the borders of Canaan, exactly answering to those we see. The ancient Egyptian artist has recorded these, as they were observed by the particular race with whom the king, in this instance, is fighting (see fig. 59); and we have selected, from the large work of Rosellini, the figure

Fig. 59.

of a man of the same race, before whom are certain hieroglyphics, which being interpreted signify the name of the tribe to which these men belong

LXXXIII.—WESTERN FIGURE ON THE GREAT ROCK TEMPLE.

(for there are four of them), namely, Tanemcho. (See Fig. 60.) Now, by converting the N in this word into an L, which change is perfectly admissible, both being liquids, we shall have a close resemblance to the word Talmai, the name of one of the three descendants of Anak, mentioned in Numbers xiii. 22, Joshua xv. 14, Judges i. 10, as head of one of the tribes inhabiting the neighbourhood of Hebron among whom the spies sent out by Moses appeared in their own sight as grasshoppers. And now when we join to this curious evidence of the hieroglyphics the peculiar fashion of their beards and hair, the tatooing, or printed marks on the skin of their arms and legs, and their gigantic stature, as represented in this particular Egyptian picture, and in the tombs of the kings from which the illustration from Rosellini is taken (see fig. 60), we shall have little difficulty in believing that we have in this picture a representation of men of the tribe of Talmai, the descendant of Anak, and with whom the Egyptians seem to have been in constant warfare.

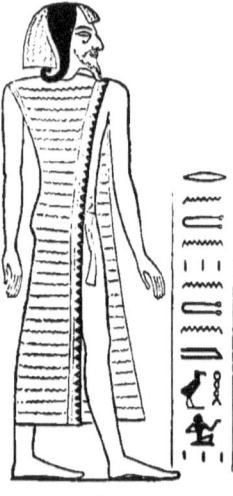

Fig. 60.

J. B.

THE CATARACT OF SAMNEH, ETHIOPIA

XXIV

PLATE LXXXIV.

The Cataract of Samneh — Ethiopia.

THE stream is here contracted between high rocky banks, and further interrupted in its course by two bold rocks, on which, in the modern engineering science, there would be little difficulty in constructing a bridge. The Nile pours furiously between these narrow channels, and there is a considerable fall on the north side.

This impediment in the stream, marking a natural boundary line, has been artificially extended on both banks, as the fragments of thick, crude brick walls indicate, in very ancient times. A small ancient temple occupies the highest point of rock on both banks, of which we shall have occasion to speak.

J. B.

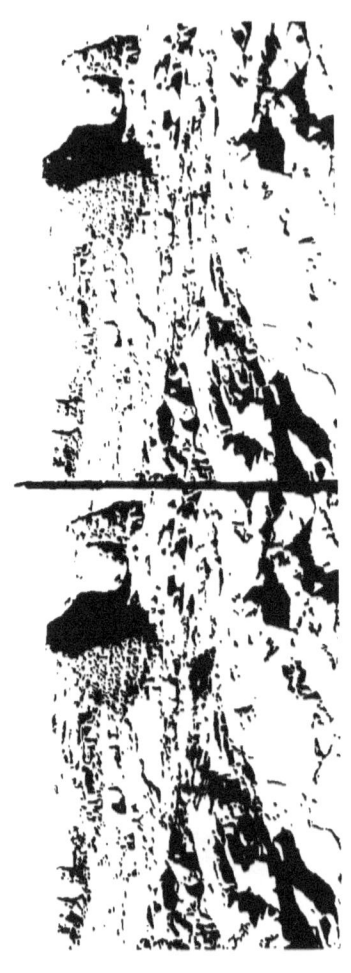

PLATE LXXXV.

The Temple of Samneh.

In this view, taken from the east bank, the crude brick remains connected with the temples can be traced on the other side of the river. Doctor Lepsius discovered inscriptions on the substructions of the temple on this bank, as well as on the scattered rocks on both banks in the neighbourhood of the temples. Many of these inscriptions were records of the highest risings of the Nile, during a series of years; and the greatest number of these records were made by the Pharaoh whom the Greeks call Mœris, and who made the labyrinth and the lake called after his name in the Faioum. Dr. Lepsius found, on comparing, the highest rise of the Nile indicated by these ancient records to be about twenty feet higher than the usual highest of the present time; and it is a curious remark of the doctor's, that these records were chiefly made by the same monarch in whose reign was accomplished that engineering contrivance in the Faioum for the irrigation of that province and those north of it in the Delta. The site of this famous artificial lake was unknown to all the Egyptian students, till a few years ago it was demonstrated and delineated by Monsieur Linant, and was, for the first time, laid down in a map of ancient Egypt, published under the auspices of the Syro-Egyptian Society of London.

J. B.

Note.—The prosperity of Samneh, and the neighbouring towns in Nubia, is explained by their neighbourhood to the Nubian gold-mines. Among the sculptures in Thebes is a procession of the subjects of King

LXXXV.—THE TEMPLE OF SAMNEH.

Thothmosis III., bringing their several tributes; and the people of Nubia and Ethiopia bring vessels of gold wrought into the form of rings. This Nubian gold made the great wealth of the great kings of Egypt, and,

Fig. 61.

of course, the towns of Nubia shared largely in it. Thothmosis III. was one of the builders at this spot, and we add a figure of his head, from a statue in the British Museum (see fig. 61).

S. S.

PLATE LXXXVI.

The Temple of Samneh — from the East.

In this view of the temple of Samneh we have some conspicuous fragments of the strong crude brick wall of the fortifications. The walls of the temple are covered with beautiful sculptures of Thothmosis III., dedicating the temple to Osirtesen III., to whom the limits, in this direction, of the Egyptian empire is to be attributed, and which he defended by massive walls from the incursions of the southern Ethiopians. The village consists of a few huts, the walls of mud, and the roof of the stalks of Indian corn and a gigantic millet. The natives cross the stream below the cataract, and in the smooth water above, on a bundle of these stalks, resembling but inferior to the ancient boat made of the papyrus.

It should have been mentioned that this anciently important production of the Nile is now nowhere to be found in Egypt. When it ceased to grow is not exactly known, but there is a curious prophetic sentence relating to its disappearance in Isaiah xix. 7.

It is said to grow in some marshy ground on the coast of Syria near Jaffa, and it certainly flourishes on the banks of a small stream near Syracuse.   J. B.

Note.—Many of the hieroglyphical inscriptions from this temple have been published from drawings made by Sir G. Wilkinson. They are far more rudely cut than the hieroglyphics in Thebes. They dedicate the temple to Thoth, the god of Ethiopia, the righteous ruler of the city of Oshmoonayn in Egypt. In the sculptures we see the god putting life into the mouth of the king, Thothmosis III., who is called the priest of Osirtesen III., and beloved by the god Knef, lord of Ethiopia.

S. S.

PLATE LXXXVII.

Rear View of the Temple at Samneh.

In this view we have a specimen of those ancient columns from which the Greek Doric shaft was derived. They are only met with in the more ancient Egyptian buildings, and in the rock-cut tombs of Benihassan. The present specimen has more facets very slightly curved than those of Benihassan, nor has it the facets corresponding with the four sides of the square abacus, flat and adorned with hieroglyphics. On the architrave stone, the hieroglyphics are of the ancient style, and on the square pier can be read the prænomen of Thothmosis III. The addition to the left is built of stone much inferior in size to the more ancient part.

Fig. 62.

A wood-cut of this kind of column is given from one in the ancient temple behind that of Tirhakah at Medinet-Habou, where it is used to obviate a weakness in the construction alluded to in the temple of Maharraka (see fig 62).

J. B.

213

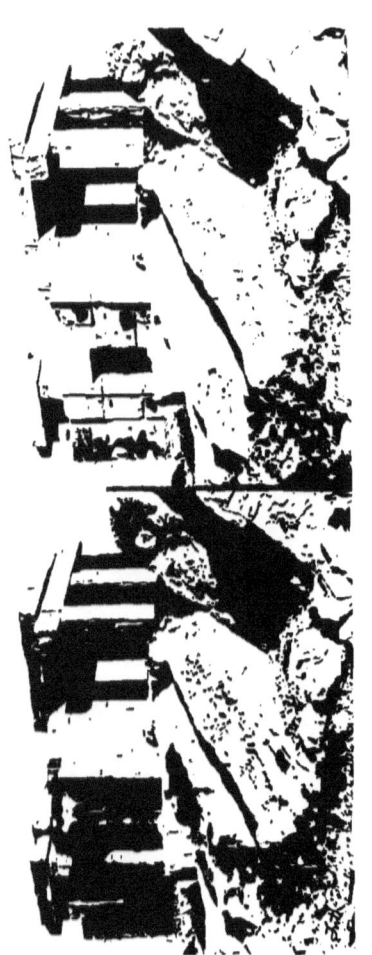

THE TEMPLE AT SÁMNÉH, ETHIOPIA

PLATE LXXXVIII.

Northern Portion of the Temple at Samneh.

In the foreground of this view of the temple of Samneh are some of the masses of stone used in the substruction of the temple and the fortifications that were attached to it. The temple has been subjected to various alterations and dilapidations, which makes it difficult to describe. Under the roof to the right, which is supported by three square piers, was buried, and nearly covered by the surrounding fragments of stone and sand, a tablet that we possess in the British Museum, the gift of the present Duke of Northumberland.

J. B.

Note.—This slab in the British Museum contains an account of the booty, ships and prisoners, taken by Amunothph III. in one of his wars, which was most likely against the tribes who dwelt to the south of Tombos.

S. S.

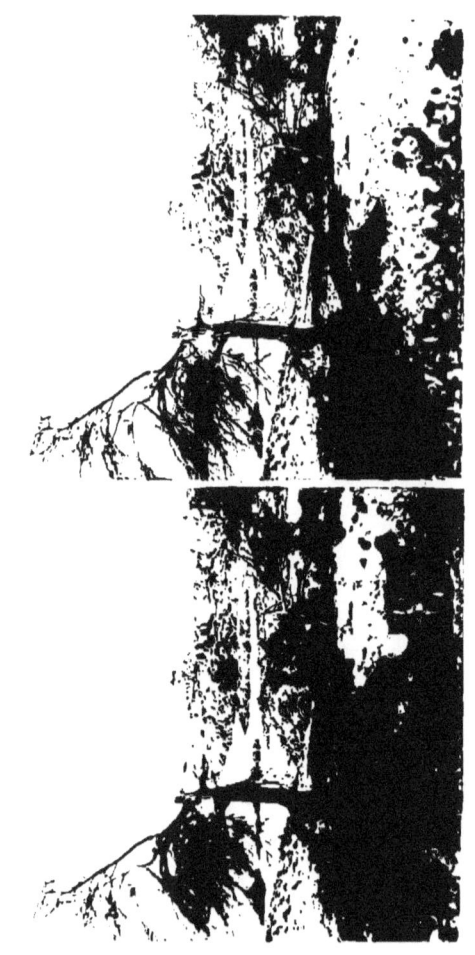

PLATE LXXXIX.

Island of Abd e' Sour.

THIS is one of the most remarkable of those rocky islands which obstruct the free passage of the stream a little above Samneh. It stands in the middle of the river, which at this part is of considerable width, and it is entirely built over with castle-like structures of crude brick, now in ruins and entirely deserted.

Whether these remains are Christian or of more ancient times, there has been no traveller to tell us. I passed it myself many years ago, hurried down by the stream in a crazy Nubian boat, which carried one of those magnificent lions presented to the nation by the present Duke of Northumberland, and it was then impossible to land. The whole of this inhospitable, picturesque country between Wady Halfa and the plains of Dongola would repay some frugal, vigorous, young, and enterprising traveller to examine.

There are towns and ruined castles in well-chosen situations on both sides of the Nile, formerly the residences of Meleks or chiefs of Arab tribes, who held a precarious, despotic sway over a very limited population and territory on this or that bank of the Nile, down to the time of the conquest of the country by Mohammed Ali, the father of the present ruler of Egypt. These buildings, like the ancient structures, have sloping walls, but many of them, as those on this island, have a solid architectural character, which induces a belief that some at least are ancient, or built on ancient foundations. The name of this island, Abd e' Sour, which means "slave of the castle," or "slave of Tyre"—probably so called from its natural and artificial strength resembling in that respect the celebrated city of that

LXXXIX.—ISLAND OF ABD E' SOUR.

name. The word Abd, in connection with Tyre, would be, in the Oriental acceptation, in the sense of resemblance to Tyre, inferior, but inheriting its qualities, as the slave resembles his master or inherits his property.

J. B.

Note.—The tree in this view is one of the acacia tribe, which gives to the country timber of very little worth and very scanty shade. Its foliage is so slight, as seen in our photograph, that it explains the proverb of the Arabs, that "Friendship in the desert is as weak and wavering as the shade of the acacia-tree."

S. S.

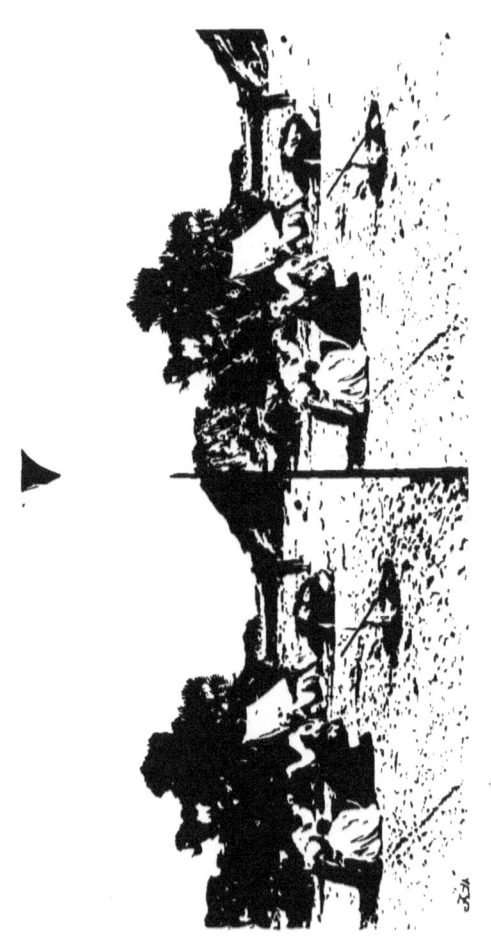

PLATE XC.

Encampment under a Doum Palm.

THE Bahr-bella-ma, or, the sea without water, as the Arabs call the desert, necessitates the Murkub-el-burr, or, the ship of the desert; and accordingly the encampment in this inhospitable spot of the sandy, rocky district of Ethiopia is properly furnished. There is no domestic animal about which such strange stories are told as the camel, even in well-accredited books of natural history. Some tell us that as soon as possible after his birth he is cruelly tortured to make him lie down in the position in which we see him in this picture; some tell us he is so vindictive in his nature, that if his master offend him, the only chance of a reconciliation between them is to make up a bundle of his master's clothes, and allow him to trample it under foot; others say he can go forty days without food or water; and it is reported by the Arabs, when the French were in Egypt, some officers, who had hired camels to take their baggage across the frontier, drove tent-pegs into their humps, on which to hang their accoutrements, and were astonished beyond measure to hear that it would be necessary to provide food for them. Whether there is not a little mixture of hyperbole in this account by an Arab chief, by way of enhancing his own superior knowledge of the habits and capability of endurance of the camel, we will not determine, but certain it is our popular acquaintance with the animal is very slender. There is not a European who does not think its neck out of all proportion, its gait awkward, its legs thin, its entire figure ugly. Herodotus thought it had an extra joint in its hind legs, and everybody supposes the callosities on its elbows and knees to be the consequence of the cruel treatment it has been subject to during its youth; and it is regarded as a semi-ferocious animal. Yet, on the contrary, there is no domestic animal more gentle or more frugal, which goes through so much fatigue, carries

XC.—ENCAMPMENT UNDER A DOUM PALM.

so great a weight with so much patience and perseverance, and at so little cost to his master, as does the camel. Rightly has he been named Gemel, the requiter: and truly, if there still exist any one of those names which Adam gave to the animals as they were marshalled before him, it is the word by which this ancient companion and fellow-labourer is still known from Morocco to India, and from India to the mountains of Ararat.

J. B.

PLATE XCI.

The Cataract of Tangour — Ethiopia.

THIS picture is very descriptive of the whole of the rocky and sandy region which extends from Wady Halfa to the island of Saye. It is only here and there, in the more favoured spots above the narrow passages of a cataract, and protected by rocks from the invasion of sand from the desert, that the Nile has time to deposit its fertilising soil over sufficient space to grow millet and corn enough for the scanty population of this wild and picturesque district. All the cataracts are less impassable during the inundation, and the smaller boats of the country do sometimes come as low as Samneh. These boats, as well as the larger, are made of planks of acacia-wood, two and three feet long, one foot wide, and three inches thick, put together like a stone wall. They have no ribs, but these planks are nailed together, and bits of rag dipped in grease are thrust between the seams, inside and out, for they have no pitch. These vessels have usually one large square sail. In the foreground is a dwarf species of the acacia; out of the wood of the taller kind these boats are made. It is the same tree which produces the gum-arabic and that sweet-scented, small, round yellow flower known as a hot-house plant. The wood is excessively hard and heavy. It is probably the same wood of which the ark was made.

In the distance are the mountains of Kolbe.

In passing the cataract of Daal, a boat, which contained one of the lions now in the British Museum, came in contact with a rock and lost its rudder.

J. B.

PLATE XCII.

Cotton-spinning at Kolbe — Ethiopia.

AT Kolbe there is a considerable extent of cultivatable land, in which cotton and millet are grown with great success. In the foreground we have a simple apparatus for weaving; and in this district of Nubia it is frequently met with in the fields, under the shade of the palm or a few mats like the present. A thick, strong piece of stuff, made of excellent cotton, twenty-five feet long, and two feet wide, was a few years ago the common currency of the country. A certain number of these were given for a sheep, a cow, or a camel. One piece cut in two, and sewn together, made the outer garment, which the natives alone know how to cast about their bodies, with a Phidian grace, like the philosophers in the Panathenaic friezes; or this piece of cloth is made up into a tunic, with ample sleeves, occasionally retained by a string passing over the shoulder, like the Parcæ of the pediment. A wider piece sometimes is worn by the women, acacia thorns serving as fibulæ, precisely like the bronze statues at Naples, or the Iris of the Parthenon, with or without a second piece serving as veil, or wrapper cast over the former dress, like in the Greek statues; for as yet neither stockings nor stays, crinolines nor gloves, are known beyond the latitude of Cairo.

J. B.

NAGY FÜRKET
XCIII

PLATE XCIII.

Wady Furket.

In the distance we see a number of small islands, which make the navigation of the river very dangerous, particularly when the river is low. In places where they are yet more crowded they form the cataracts. In the foreground the rounded form of the rocks, with the evident marks of the action of water upon them, tells us that we are in the sandstone formation; while the sharp points of the hills beyond as clearly show that they belong to the granite which bursts through the sandstone in a variety of places, and forms the cataracts. We are here in a range of country about one hundred miles long, between Wady Halfa and the Island of Saye, in which the granite and sandstone alternate too frequently for us to distinguish and count the cataracts accurately. It may be best considered as the long granite district of the second cataract.

A hasty glance at the geology of the valley will not be uninteresting.— (1st.) The Delta, below Cairo, is alluvial soil. (2nd.) At the pyramids on one side, and the Mocattam hills on the other, begin the two ranges of limestone between which the Nile flows. (3rd.) At Silsilis, as we go up the river, the rocks on both sides change to sandstone, and the valley becomes narrower. (4th.) At Syene we meet with a granite range which forms the first cataract. (5th.) We then travel over the sandstone again, passing by the quarries, till we come to the granite which forms the second cataract a little above Abou Simbel. (6th.) This district of one hundred miles in length, of alternately sandstone and granite, forms a number of small cataracts too numerous to distinguish. (7th.) At the Island of Saye we come to another sandstone district, in which is the town of Soleb. (8th.) At Tombos we come to another mass of granite which forms the third cataract.

XCIII.—WADY FURKET.

(9th.) We then, in the bend of the river, have a long district of sandstone, which ends soon after passing Napata, once the capital city of Ethiopia. (10th.) Then we come to the granite of the fourth cataract. (11th.) Then we have another sandstone district of eighty miles; and at Abou Hammed (12th) we come to the granite of the fifth cataract.

Here we leave our geological sketch, as we have for some time passed the limits of Mr. Frith's interesting photographic journey.

S. S.

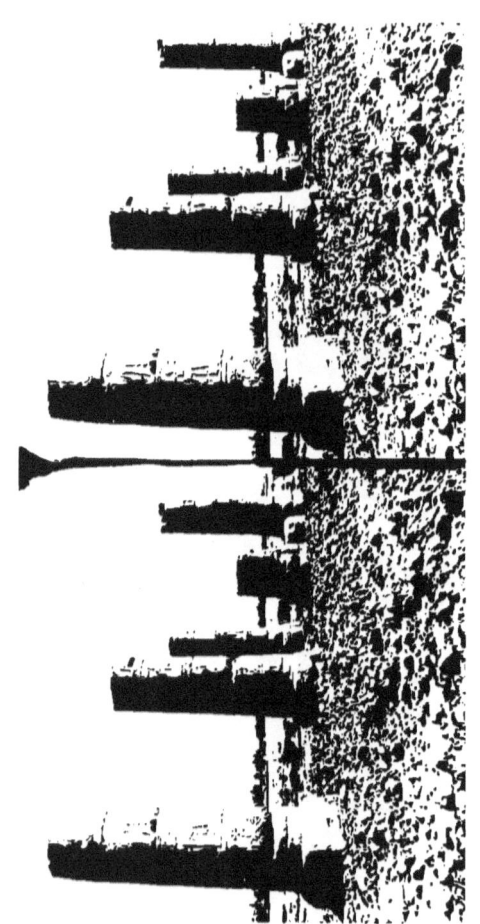

PLATE XCIV.

Columns of the Temple at Amara — Ethiopia.

AMARA is the name of a village on the eastern bank of the Nile, near to which is a small ruin consisting of six columns, without capitals, and some fragments of others, but no walls. The sculpture on these columns is in a style that may be termed Ethiopian, like that of Meroe.

The fat figures of the king and queen, who are making the offerings to Amun, and Athor, and other divinities of Egypt, are on the shaded side of the columns, and therefore not seen. The sculptures, particularly the hieroglyphics, have never been finished. In the lower compartment of the column are figures of Nilus, carrying two water vessels, out of which issue two streams. The bases of these columns are square. These ruins belong to an Ethiopian dynasty that erected some considerable buildings in Meroe, and affected the Egyptian style of architecture with an admixture of Roman. The queen on these buildings of Meroe appears as the principal personage, as she does in the small temples attached to the pyramids of Napata. The hieroglyphics are badly formed and illegible.

May the queen whom we see on these monuments have been the mistress of the eunuch whom Philip baptized, and hence the establishment of Christianity in Ethiopia, of which we have seen so many indications in the ancient temples?

J. B.

COLUMNS OF THE TEMPLE AT AMARA, ETHIOPIA

PLATE XCV.

Near View of the Columns of the Temple at Amara—Ethiopia.

THERE is considerable cultivation and numerous date-trees along the borders of the river. The ruin is situated on the edge of the desert, which is here formed of low conglomerate rocks, and little or no sand.

J. B.

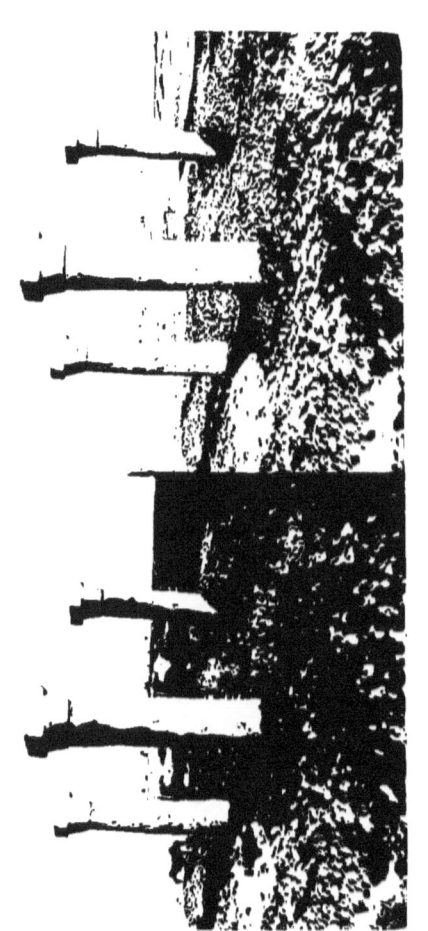

PLATE XCVI.

Granite Columns on the Island of Saye—Ethiopia.

SAYE is a large island just above the stony region that begins at Wady Halfa, and terminates here. There are the remains of a temple of Thothmosis III. and Amunothph II., which most likely furnished the materials for this Christian building. There is still a considerable population on the island, and granite, fashioned into columns, indicates a prosperity that does not exist in any class of the community at the present time. Some years ago there were four bronze cannons lying on the beach of the west coast of this island, said to have been brought there by the Mamelukes. In the distance is a remarkable mountain, called Gebel Abeer.

J. B.

NOTE.—As it is highly improbable that heavy stones were ever carried far up the river against the stream, we conclude that in every case they were brought from the quarries next above the spot where we now find them. Hence we may suppose that these columns were cut into shape in the large granite quarries which Lepsius found at Kerman, near the island of Tombos, at the third cataract. In the same quarries were probably made the two fine lions which were presented to the British Museum by Lord Prudhoe, now the Duke of Northumberland.

S. S.

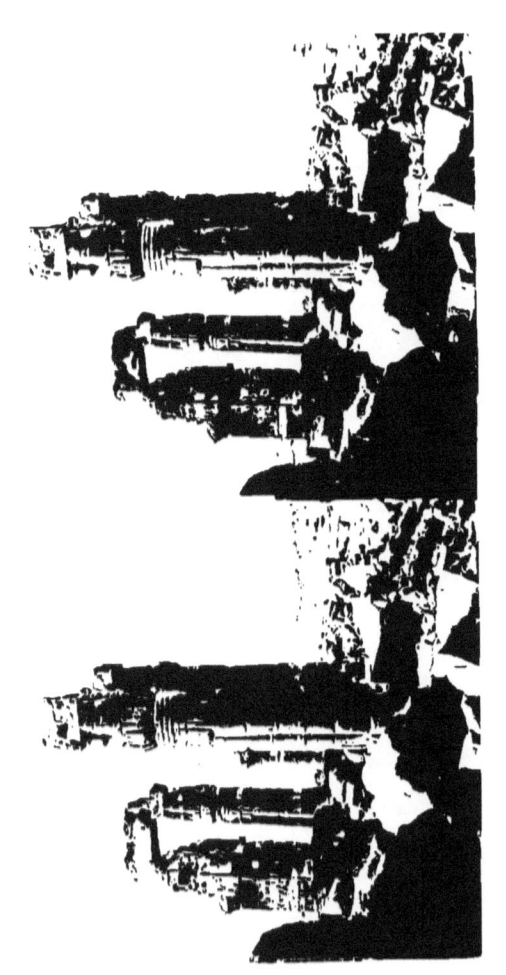

THE COLUMNS OF AMUNOTHPH III AT SOB B-ETHIOPIA

XCVII

PLATE XCVII.

Column of Amunothph iii. at Soleb — Ethiopia.

SOLEB is situated on the west bank of the Nile, about 700 miles in a straight line from the Mediterranean. This magnificent ruin is some little distance from the river, and stands on elevated ground. It is approached between two rows of ram-headed sphinxes, with the bodies of lions, like those in sandstone of the dromos of Luxor; but these are of granite, now almost entirely perished. Then a magnificent pylon, which was formerly flanked by the usual truncated pyramids; then a court surrounded by columns of the ancient order, formed of eight papyrus-buds, bound together like those of Luxor, and of equally elegant proportions. To this court succeeded a second of inferior dimensions, but also surrounded by a portico, and to this a chamber, probably a hall of columns. Here, on the bases of six columns, are the names of conquered provinces, represented by the upper part of a man, surmounting a dentated or turreted oval, in which are the hieroglyphics representing the sound of the word constituting the name of the province or city. These names have all been published by Dr. Lepsius in the great work of the Prussian Mission.

This temple was erected by Amunothph III., about 1250 B.C., and dedicated to Amun-ra, the chief divinity of Thebes.

The triangularity of the stalk of the papyrus is well defined by the shadow on both the nearer and more distant columns; in short, it may be said every leading characteristic of the natural plant is produced in the stone imitation, consistent with its application to the support of the architrave and roof-stones; and there exists between the capital and shaft

XCVII.—COLUMN OF AMUNOTIIPH III. AT SOLEB—ETHIOPIA.

a common-sense analogy, which, it must be confessed, does not obtain between the capital and shaft of the Corinthian order. Fig. 63 is shown as a column formed of a cluster of stalks of the papyrus.

J. B.

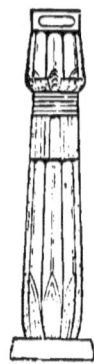

Fig. 63.

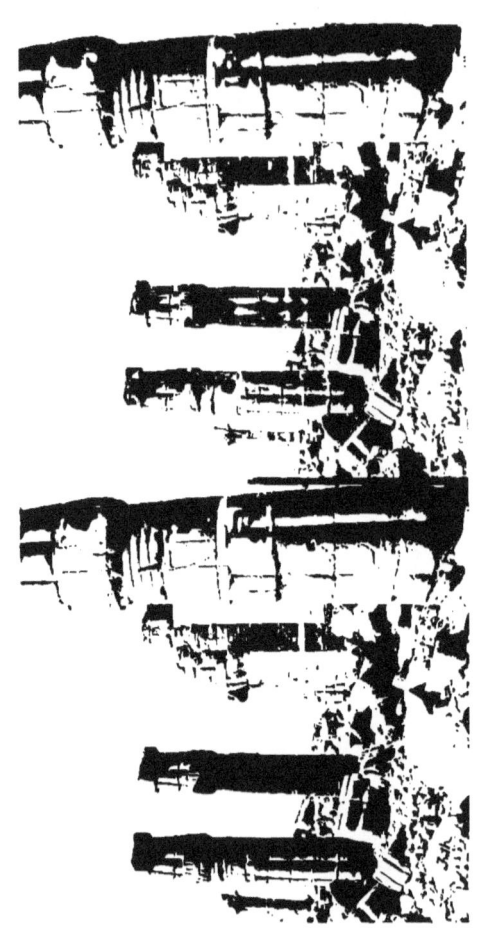

PLATE XCVIII.

General View of Columns of Amunothph iii. at Soleb.

In this view is a column with a capital, representing a palm, by no means usual in the temples of the age of the Pharaohs, although very common in those of the Ptolemaic and Roman periods. It is by no means improbable that many of the varieties of capitals we admire in the more recent temples of Greek and Roman times were copied from more ancient examples, which had been nearly destroyed at the time of the Babylonian and Persian invasions, and entirely disappeared since.

This has been the fate of the beautiful portico of Ashmoonayn, which was composed of a variety of columns, of which we have no specimen now left. This temple of Soleb probably at one time served as a Christian place of worship; but now it is the habitation of wolves and foxes.

J. B.

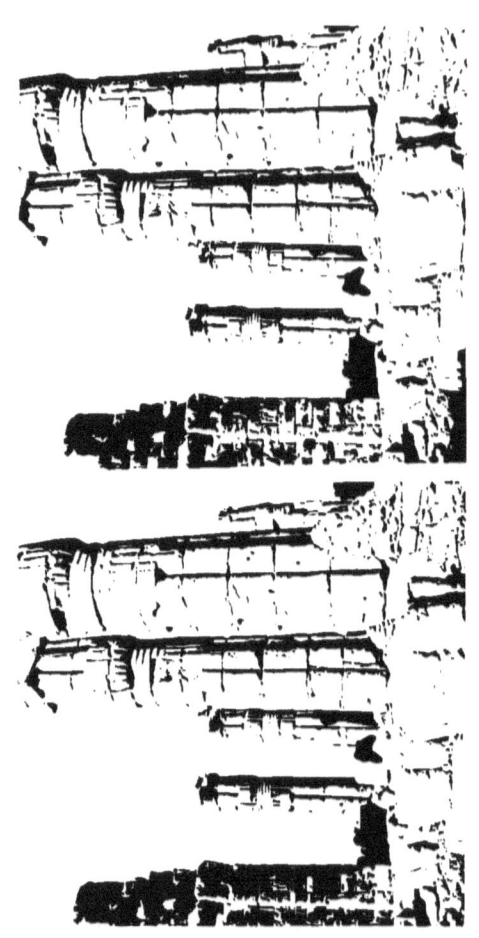

PLATE XCIX.

View of the Column of Amunothph iii. at Soleb, from the East.

NEARER view of the columns and door-jamb of the first court. The five bands under the bud of the papyrus, the strips, bound together likewise by five bands, that pass under the five bands at the neck of the capital, and appear again between each stalk, are clearly defined in this view; but the finer lines, representing the leaves, envelope the bud at its base, and those that envelope the base of the stalk cannot be discovered in any of the columns, because they are much defaced both by time and accident, and likewise by the constant beating of the coarse sand by the violent and almost constant winds.

We have, however, given a woodcut of the elegant specimen in granite we possess in our national collection of a column of this order, and of the same age as those of Soleb.

J. B.

NOTE.—These beautiful columns, of the time of Amunothph III., of the coarse sandstone of the neighbourhood, tell us by their workmanship that the country was at that time quietly ruled over by the kings of Thebes, under whose rule the whole valley below the third cataract was most rich and prosperous. Such a temple could only have been raised at a time when the laws were quietly obeyed and the machinery of government working with full regularity. The Egyptian sway in his reign reached to the third cataract, where the granite quarries were worked for the statues in the

XCIX.—VIEW OF THE COLUMN OF AMUNOTHPH III. AT SOLEB.

temples above the quarries at the first cataract. Rameses II., the most powerful of the Egyptian kings, stretched his arms yet farther south, and built at Napata, near the fourth cataract. But that is beyond the limit of our views. The buildings beyond Soleb are in worse taste, and are less interesting, and are not often visited by travellers.

S. S.

PLATE C.

Soleb, looking from the Inner Court towards the Gate.

This photograph is a masterpiece of effect. In magnificent *chiaro scuro*, and picturesque confusion are some masses of stone, among which is the base of one of those columns on which were sculptured the ovals, already described, containing, in pronounceable hieroglyphics, the names of conquered provinces or cities. The block here spoken of is that of cylindrical shape, immediately under the three columns to the right. On it may be distinctly seen an oval surmounted by the upper part of the figure of an Asiatic, with his arms tied behind him, and his face turned towards the spectator.

The next block produces a long shadow, modified in its form by the undulations of the sand over which it is cast; and quite in the left-hand corner of the picture are three blocks piled up on each other, exhibiting a variety of surface and fracture, perfectly descriptive of the nature and quality of the fine white gritstone of which a great part of this temple is built.

From this ruin it has been conjectured that those two fine lions, the ornament of the Egyptian saloon of the British Museum, were taken by an Ethiopian prince to adorn the principal temple at Napata, now called Gebel Berkel, whence the present Duke of Northumberland caused them to be transported to this country.

J. B.

Note.—The reader will have seen, in the foregoing plates, and also in the wood-cuts, that the oval in which the king's name is written has a foot

C.—SOLEB, LOOKING FROM THE INNER COURT TOWARDS THE GATE.

or flat ground on which it may be said to stand. It is the side view of a signet ring standing on the engraved surface, and having the writing placed in the hollow through which the finger should pass. But the oval in this photograph, on which is written the name of the conquered country, has no such stand or foot. It is a shield held in the hand of a prisoner, who figuratively represents his nation.

S. S.

THE END.

www.ingramcontent.com/pod-product-compliance
Lightning Source LLC
Chambersburg PA
CBHW020525300426
44111CB00008B/542